The High Performance Heart

The High Performance Heart

Effective Training for Health, Fitness and Competition with the Heart Rate Monitor

Dr. Philip Maffetone
and
Matthew Mantell

With a foreword by Mark Allen

Bicycle Books – San Francisco

Printed in the United States of America

Published by:
Bicycle Books, Inc.
1282 - 7th Avenue
San Francisco, CA 94122
U.S.A.

Distributed to the book trade by:
USA: National Book Network, Lanham, MD
Canada: Raincoast Book Distribution, Vancouver, BC
UK: Chris Lloyd Sales and Marketing Services, Poole, Dorset

Cover: Design and photographs by Kent Lytle
               Bicycle and cycling dress courtesy A Bicycle Odyssey, Sausalito
               Tennis dress courtesy Love-30, San Anselmo

Frontispiece:
               Triathlete Mike Pigg in action on the bike
               (photo courtesy Polar)

Publisher's Cataloging in Publication Data
Maffetone, Philip B.
The High Performance Heart : effective training for competition, health
and fitness with the heart rate monitor / Philip Maffetone and Matthew
Mantell. – 2nd. fully updated and expanded ed.
        p.   cm.

Includes bibliographical references (p.) and index.
ISBN 0-933201-64-8

1. Athletes—Health and hygiene. 2. Heart rate monitoring. 3. Physical
education and training. 4. Exercise—physiological aspects. I Mantell,
Matthew. II. Title.

RC1236.H43M34 1994   613.7'11–dc20

Library of Congress Catalog Card No. 94-72463

To Lillian
M.E.M.

To everybody pursuing both health *and* fitness
P.M.

Acknowledgements

For her tireless research assistance, we owe thanks to Kathryn Silberger, librarian at Marist College in Poughkeepsie, New York. Also, we are extremely grateful for the editorial help and support provided by Rob van der Plas, our editor at Bicycle Books. A special tip of the bike cap goes to Jonathan Sternfield, a longtime friend and co-conspirator.

Foreword by Mark Allen

The heart rate monitor is the most significant tool in my training program. That's why I use it during every workout. The information the monitor provides has helped me improve my athletic performance each year, for the past decade.

While the heart rate monitor is really a simple device, it's a powerful one, also. Unfortunately, some athletes don't have the patience to monitor their heart rate. But they are the people who are missing out on reaching their full athletic potential. A heart rate monitor helps you to train smart, utilize your workout time better, and get the best performance from your body.

Yet, just because you use a monitor doesn't necessarily mean you're using the device correctly. For example, take the 220 minus age, target zone formula. This procedure fails to consider either the health or fitness of an athlete. And unless you factor in both of these aspects, your target zone won't be very accurate.

To achieve the precision I require for training, I utilize the 180 target zone formula. The reason many athletes are afraid to use this system is because they are not familiar with it. All I can say is that it is the most accurate way to maintain health and fitness.

On the subjects of diet, the target zone, as well as training and competing, Phil is a little bit ahead of his time. Maybe the medical community and the public will catch up with him in 5 or 10 years. By reading *The High Performance Heart*, you won't have to wait anywhere near that long.

Mark Allen
Five-time Ironman Triathlon winner and
record-holder for the fastest time (1993)

"I use the heart rate monitor every day in training, and on the bike during the Ironman race. It allows me to be more precise, prevent injury and raise my performance."

Mark Allen, 5-time Ironman Triathlon winner

"The heart rate monitor has been my training companion for years. Without it, I'd still be injured and would not have the success I now enjoy."

Colleen Cannon, Triathlon champion

"The heart rate provides the most readily obtainable and concrete data about an athlete's fitness. This makes the heart rate monitor an essential tool for any cyclist."

Alexander Kuznetsov, coach of the LocoSphinx club based in St. Petersburg (formerly Leningrad) and the Soviet amateur team at the 1991–1994 Tour Du Pont.

by **Massimo Testa, MD**

*Physician to the Motorola bicycle racing team,
director of the Milan Sport Medicine Research Center*

When Andy Hampsten won the hardest uphill time trial of the 1988 Giro d'Italia, he became the first American overall winner in the race's history. Many observers were intrigued by the flexible strap that was visible under his aerodynamic skin suit; they later learned he was wearing a heart rate monitor to keep track of his physical performance.

At that time, the use of a heart rate monitor was still quite uncommon, even in professional bicycle racing circles. Since then, what was once a novelty has become a widely used tool in competition and training. In fact, most top athletes and their coaches have discovered that the heart rate monitor is the ideal instrument to increase the efficiency of the athlete's training and competitive effort.

Now, at last, here is the book that shows the "ordinary" amateur athlete how to get the same benefits as the professionals on the major teams. This book by my friends Dr. Philip Maffetone and Matthew Mantell explains how to use the heart rate monitor for effective training, whether for fitness or competition. In a logical step-by-step process this book explains how to go about choosing the equipment and how to use it to maximum advantage. The book develops all the important aspects of scientific training methods to achieve a personalized training program based on the use of the HRM. I am sure this book will help you improve your athletic performance while maximizing health and fitness.

Through my experience as a physician to professional bicycle racing teams, I have become convinced that the heart rate is the most precise parameter to evaluate an athlete's physical performance outside the physiology laboratory. The heart rate monitor provides the accurate and instantaneous feedback that allows the informed and intelligent athlete to optimize his or her efforts, whether training for competition or fitness.

Working with both amateur and professional endurance athletes has convinced me that the subjective feeling of fatigue is not always an accurate index for developing an optimal, personalized training program. The heart rate, on the other hand, is a valuable and objective means of determining the athlete's responses and adaptations to every workload situation. It also helps test the athlete's aerobic efficiency under different conditions, providing valuable information to establish the most effective training techniques, the most efficient riding style, or to fine-tune the bike or other equipment.

For the recreational athlete, the heart rate monitor can also be an invaluable source of information. It prevents "weekend warriors" from exceeding their limits, thus endangering their health in pursuit of fitness.

For exercise programs dealing with cardiac rehabilitation or weight reduction, the ability to monitor the workout level is very important. Patients recovering from a heart attack or heart surgery can maintain the target zone recommended by their cardiologist. Overweight patients adhering to a regimen of proper diet and aerobic exercise can use the heart rate monitor during their workout sessions to make sure they are metabolizing fats.

Clearly, the heart rate monitor has the potential to revolutionize training for health, fitness and competition. I can't emphasize enough how important it is to get a correct understanding of the subject across to athletes and fitness-conscious people everywhere. The authors of *The High Performance Heart* have done an excellent job of demystifying the subject. I am confident this book will prove invaluable to all who strive for fitness and health.

Table of Contents

Chapter 1

The Difference Between Fitness and Health

In 1976, I was lying in a hospital bed with an undiagnosed illness watching the Summer Olympic Games on television. My weight had dropped to 98 pounds—and I am 6 feet tall. I was so weak that I couldn't turn the TV on. A nurse had to come into the room and do that for me.

As I started to watch the Olympic sprinters, I recalled my own track career and the ease of flight when I was a national-class runner in college. And here I was confined to a hospital bed, hardly able to move.

Eventually, I recovered from the illness and started to do a lot of walking. As I got stronger and stronger, I wanted to find a measure of fitness to prove to myself that I was healthy. For a while, I didn't know what to do.

Then, in April of 1980, I was watching television and saw the runners who were finishing the Boston Marathon. These people are really healthy, I thought to myself; they just ran 26 miles. Maybe this is what I can do to prove I'm healthy, too.

Back then, the New York Marathon was held in October. I felt that if I had 6 months to train, I'd have enough time to enter that event. That's what I did.

When the cannon went off at the starting line, I ran the first few miles of the marathon with a feeling of exhilaration. At the 10-mile point, I still felt wonderful. But, as I crossed over the Queensborough bridge and came down on to First Avenue—

which was around 15 miles into the race, I began to crave cotton candy. I also had cramps and was talking to myself.

By the 18th mile, I sat down on a curb in Harlem—totally incoherent. After a while, my head cleared. It was then that I caught sight of my original goal: To finish the race in order to prove I was healthy.

Suddenly, I noticed that two men from an ambulance service were walking toward me. I was certain they wanted to put me on the stretcher and cart me away. But I wasn't going to allow that to happen. It would have stopped me from confirming I was healthy. So I forced myself to get up and run again.

When I finally arrived in Central Park, I started to weave—and ran into a television camera man. I don't remember anything else about those last few miles of the marathon. However, I do recall that after I crossed the finish line, someone hung a medal around my neck to signify I had completed the event. I began to cry.

The next thing I knew, I woke up on a cot in the medical tent designated for the injured and ill marathon finishers. A nurse handed me a cup of coffee and a doughnut. As I consumed this stuff, I heard people moaning, groaning, and crying in pain. I saw others entering and leaving the tent on stretchers. There were doctors and nurses rushing from one person to another to administer IVs. As I observed this scene, I said to myself, "Every runner in here—including me—has finished the New York Marathon. So, it indeed proves we are all fit."

It was then that I realized there was a very big difference between health and fitness. Sure, I was fit enough to have finished the marathon, but along with the other athletes in the emergency tent, I was not in a good state of health.

In the remaining chapters of the book, we'll explore how to be fit *without* sacrificing your health.

Chapter 2

The Heart Rate as the Basis for Scientific Training

Today, training and competing in virtually all athletic disciplines has become quite systematic, if not truly scientific. This is a far cry from the not so distant past when folklore and tradition prevailed.

One quaint custom held by many coaches and trainers in the 1950s was that athletes should never drink water during their workouts. To do so, in their opinion, would sap a player's

Fig. 2.1. Early HRM: handlebar-mounted unit with a sensor belt that can be worn over light clothing. (photo courtesy Polar)

mental toughness. Even when temperatures broke the century mark, the water bucket appeared only after practice. Burly football players were not the only athletes forced to adhere to this convention. It was also applied to whippet-like long distance runners. As late as the 1976 Olympic Games, there was a rule prohibiting the consumption of any fluids during the first 6 miles of the marathon.

Today, no self-respecting coach, trainer, or athletic governing body would sanction such a primitive and physically dangerous policy. Most notably, this revised thinking about consuming fluids is underscored in almost all training manuals. For example, virtually all cycling manuals now encourage riders to sip from their water bottles every 15 minutes—even when they don't feel thirsty. Failure to so, say the experts, could ultimately lead to dehydration.

While rehydration is no longer an issue, the same cannot be said for another time-honored sports tradition: the "no pain, no gain" philosophy. Proponents of this crude concept believe that if athletes do not hurt while working out, they stand little chance of making any progress.

Although the "no pain, no gain" attitude has lost some ground, it continues to fight a rearguard action. That's because even the most enlightened athletes can be filled with doubt as to whether or not they are practicing hard enough.

Certainly no one would dispute the notion that hard work and dedication are two prerequisites for making advances in training and competition. But when elite and recreational athletes take this exercise tandem to the extreme, there frequently are dire consequences: burnout and overtraining, which can lead to a loss of enthusiasm for an activity, as well as illness and injury.

Yet, regardless of your level of ability, you can avoid these pitfalls. To do so, you need an intelligently designed exercise program that remains sensitive to your mind and body. Furthermore, to reach your full potential in training and competition, it is essential to obtain objective, individualized information.

For the modern athlete, one of the best means of acquiring this crucial data is by using a *heart rate monitor* (HRM). Although the HRM is a relatively new tool in the field of athletics, it has a long history in the medical profession. For decades, doctors have used various types of HRMs to keep tabs on patients afflicted with cardiac disorders.

By monitoring the heart rate, an athlete is provided with information that will improve the efficiency of his or her body.

Fig. 2.2. The heart rate monitor is useful for indoor exercise studios as well as in outdoor activities such as cycling and running. (photo courtesy Sensor Dynamics)

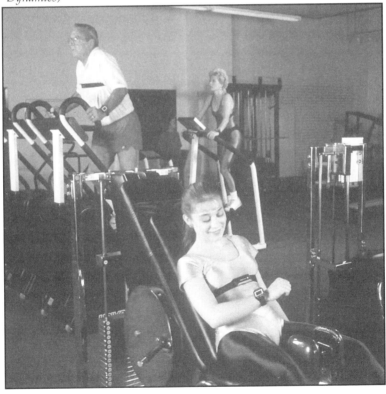

That's because in one sense, the heart rate functions like your car's tachometer. As you drive away from a green light, the tachometer registers the engine's increasing revolutions per minute. Similarly, when your body works harder during exercise, the heart reveals this effort through an increasing number of beats per minute. Moreover, just as a race car driver employs a tachometer to improve his machine's performance, you, too, can use your heart rate—in conjunction with an HRM—to gauge, as well as optimize, your health and fitness.

A common fallacy held by both active and sedentary people is that good health and optimum fitness are synonymous. But as it turns out, that is not correct. Your fitness is measured by the ability to perform a physical task—which can range from an hour of leisurely riding or walking to competing in the Tour de France or running a marathon. Good health has nothing to do with athletic ability. Rather, it's a state where all your bodily systems are functioning harmoniously.

It's not unusual, then, to find athletes who are very fit, yet are in a poor state of health at the same time. An example of this condition is the cyclist who breezes through daily workouts and is still plagued by colds or nagging injuries. (This all too common circumstance is indicative of an imbalanced training program—which can be restored to equilibrium through the correct use of an HRM.)

Worse yet is the recent spate of world-class athletes who have succumbed to heart attacks. Their ranks include running guru Jim Fixx, basketball sharpshooters Hank Gathers, Pete Maravich and Reggie Lewis, as well as several European professional bicycle racers.

Invariably, such tragedies are so shocking that many people begin to reflect on the quality of their lives. But all too often the impact soon fades, and then it's back to business as usual: jobs and personal relationships that induce excessive stress; diets that don't provide adequate nourishment or that foster weight problems. Generally, people who remain on a course that diminishes their health believe a heart attack—or another type of physical problem—is something that happens to someone else.

As a person who is already physically active, you are already on the road to a healthy lifestyle. This book is geared to help you achieve this eminently worthwhile objective. Its central premise is quite simple: The heart rate monitor, which is both sophisticated and user-friendly, can be used effectively to improve your overall well-being. By virtue of its precision, it can maintain the all-important symmetry of your training program. So, whether you are a fitness enthusiast or a competitive athlete, an HRM can take you to higher levels of health and conditioning.

This book explains how to evaluate an HRM's strengths and weaknesses, how the various devices function, and which models are the most appropriate for either fitness or competition.

Most important, the book reveals how to accurately calculate your individual *heart rate target zone*. By exercising within this boundary, you can attain superior conditioning and reduce the chances of sustaining debilitating illnesses or injuries. However, should you experience either of these problems, you will learn how to facilitate your rehabilitation. Morover, this book shows how to apply your target zone data to both aerobic and anaerobic workouts—the two necessary exercise activities required to maintain and balance your health and fitness.

While bicycle racing is certainly one athletic discipline where the heart rate monitor has been used quite effectively (and indeed most of the examples in this book are based on cycling), cyclists are not the only athletes who can profit from this book. You will be shown how the training and competitive principles related to the HRM can be utilized by runners and swimmers, as well as by triathletes and biathletes. Given that the most modern HRMs are both reliable and affordable, it's the wise athlete who incorporates this device into his or her training program. Ultimately, this technology can provide a physiological window that will enable you to evaluate, control and promote your health and conditioning.

Chapter 3

A Brief History of the MAF Training Program

Biofeedback, as defined by *Dorland's Medical Dictionary*, is a priceless method of providing auditory—or visual—evidence to an individual about their body's function so that they may exert control over that function. This kind of activity was rapidly becoming popular for research and therapy when I was studying to become a doctor during the mid-1970s. And through my own investigations into the field of biofeedback, I immediately saw how it could be applied to sports—a subject I had been involved in as an athlete.

What I realized then was that the pulse or heart rate would be an excellent way for an athlete to get biofeedback during training and competing. In this sports application, biofeedback could control the quality of an exercise.

So, throughout 1977 and 1978, I began using manual pulse-taking as a means of gathering objective information in order to individualize a person's exercise program. One thing, however, made this very difficult, as well as relatively inaccurate: The exerciser had to continually slow down or—worse yet—stop to check his or her heart rate. Still, I gradually saw important relationships between the quality of training and specific heart rates. As a result of these observations, I started to create programs whereby athletes could base the intensity of their workouts on the heart rate changes during these efforts.

My research to develop precision in this endeavor led me to compare manual pulse taking with pulse meters. These devices measured the heart rate by means of a sensor clamped to the exerciser's finger or earlobe, but it turned out to be impossible for most athletes to get reliable readings with it.

Around 1979, a heart monitor appeared on the market that would measure the heart rate from the chest wall. The new monitor was particularly valuable when I took runners to the track for training. Not only could I see changes in their gaits, but I could more accurately compare these observations to changes in their heart rates.

By 1981, I had created a training program based on using the heart rate monitor as a biofeedback mechanism. This program focused on health as well as fitness. It also specified various levels of aerobic and anaerobic workouts.

As time went on, this training program became more re-fined. It could be used to correlate blood lactate and oxygen uptake with heart rate. Then I discovered a formula to deter-mine maximum aerobic heart rates that was an accurate rep-resentation of what athletes would learn if they went to a lab for evaluation. This formula was quite different from the standard 220 minus age procedure. It differentiated between chronological age and physiological age, and took into ac-count an athlete's overall health.

Early in 1982, I developed the Maximum Aerobic Function test, or MAF. Originally, I called this the Maximum Aerobic Pace, or MAP, because I had used it to evaluate the pace of runners on a track. But MAP was already a term being em-ployed in physiology as an acronym for Maximum Aerobic Power. So, it was suggested the test be dubbed MAF because I had been working with it to measure other athletic activities or functions—such as miles per hour in cycling or distance in swimming—besides time in running.

Chapter 4

A Matter of Balance: Aerobic and Anaerobic

While most athletes toss around the words *aerobic* and *anaerobic* as casually as their bike, swimming goggles or running shoes, they usually don't understand what these terms really mean. They commonly say that aerobic means using oxygen, or the breathing pattern that accompanies long, steady exercising. Anaerobic is described as a state lacking oxygen—such as when ascending a steep hill, where breathing becomes extremely difficult.

These pedestrian definitions, which are neither accurate nor precise, were originated, in part, by microbiologists. Since some laboratory microbes required oxygen to live, researchers classified them as *aerobic*. Those microbes that couldn't survive in oxygen were, therefore, designated *anaerobic*.

Both of these nomenclatures are fine for microbes, but they hardly apply to people who run, swim or ride bicycles. Obviously, oxygen is essential for all of life's activities. Yet even the most well-conditioned athlete would be hard pressed to remain in a state void of oxygen for much more than a couple of minutes. In regard to aerobic and anaerobic, then, laboratory definitions definitely don't apply to human beings.

For the athlete, useful explanations of these two exercise patterns are instructive as well as significant. The most obvious distinction between aerobic and anaerobic activity is the different kinds of fuel they rely on. Aerobic workouts, for the most part, utilize fat (fatty acids) as a source of energy, while anaerobic efforts are fueled by sugar (glucose). Consequently, the most practical meaning of each term is this: aerobic is the chemical state when the body is burning fat, and anaerobic is the state when it burns sugar.

It is important to note that when you are burning sugar, you are not burning fat. Frequently, your body is storing fat.

Generally, the aerobic process, which relies on slow-twitch muscle fibers, contributes to your good health. It improves the heart's condition as well as blood circulation; it helps the body regulate fats and the hormonal system, and it enhances physical endurance. The anaerobic process cannot provide you with any of these benefits. That's because it is usually a product of intense exertion or competition which primarily involves an athlete's fast-twitch muscle fibers.

Table 4.1. Percentage of aerobic and anaerobic energy during maximal exercise.

Duration	Percent Aerobic	Percent Anaerobic
10 sec.	10	90
60 sec.	30	70
2 min.	50	50
4 min.	65	35
10 min.	85	15
30 min.	95	5
60 min.	98	2
2 hrs.	99	1

Source: Astrand, P. and K. Rodahl. *Textbook of Work Physiology.*

The obvious question, then, is how do you determine whether your workouts are aerobic or anaerobic? Simple: check your pulse with an HRM. Fluctuations in an athlete's heart rate occur simultaneously with changes in other bodily functions. As the pulse rises during a workout, there is a parallel increase in oxygen uptake (the amount of O_2 utilized), the rate of breathing, and lactic acid, or blood lactate, buildup.

While you are pedaling your bike or running at a comfortable aerobic pace, for example, your heart rate will probably remain at a relatively low level. In this easy exercise mode, the body derives most of its energy from fat. But later in the workout, you may start to really hammer. As your cadence

Fig. 4.1. Nelson Vails' specialty is the short sprint race, essentially all anaerobic. In preparation and training for this kind of event, the heart rate monitor should play an important role. But this is one discipline in which the heart rate monitor is generally not used during the actual event.

gets progressively faster, your heart rate begins to rise and, as a result, more and more fuel is required. When the body reaches a point where it can no longer obtain energy from fat, it shifts to sugar for its fuel source. (The body converts sugar into energy faster than it converts fat.) Beyond this point, the body is functioning anaerobically.

It is especially difficult for most athletes—regardless of their sport—to recognize when they have turned anaerobic. And after they have made this transition, it's not easy for them to get back into the aerobic state again. That's because the increase in lactic acid associated with anaerobic activity tends to suppress the body's aerobic functioning. So once you have become even mildly anaerobic, you will obtain considerably fewer aerobic benefits.

Consequently, you should not overlook the fact that, depending on your workout regimen, you are *training* the body to become either predominantly anaerobic or aerobic. Indeed, this conditioning impression molded during exercise continues, through a complex biochemical process, for as long as 48 hours after exercise.

Given all of the above information, it's a good bet that athletes who are continually in the throes of illness or injury may be spending too much time working out anaerobically.

To achieve the necessary balance between the aerobic (fat-burning) and anaerobic (sugar-burning) states, it's essential to employ an HRM. But, in order to utilize this exercise device correctly, you must first establish your personal heart rate level. This critical information can literally be a lifesaver.

Chapter 5

Determining Your Heart Rate

Until recently, most athletes still relied on an antiquated, manual method for gauging their heart rate, and too many still do so today. During and after training, they place an index finger on the neck's carotid artery. Then they employ either the 6- or 10-second formula in hopes of determining their heart rate in bpm. (The former prescription calls for counting your heart rate for 6 seconds and multiplying by 10; the latter requires counting the beats for 10 seconds and multiplying by

Fig. 5.1 Inside the sports physiology lab: Elite triathlete Mike Pigg on the treadmill to measure his Respiratory Quotient in order to determine the correct composition of his sports drink.

6.) Certainly, this procedure is quite simple—but as for being accurate, that's an entirely different matter.

In order to take your pulse by hand, you must at least slow down. If nothing else, the termination or reduction of your workout pace means you are not measuring the *working* heart rate. As a result of this circumstance, the figure produced by both the 6- and 10-second methods can be off by as much as 10 to 15 bpm.

There are several common scenarios guaranteed to create unreliable manual heart rate readings. In the case of cycling, these include hill climbs and sprinting as well as performing speed work and intervals.

Let's take, for example, climbing a hill on a hot summer day. It is 90 degrees in the shade, and you have just crested the summit of a tough ascent. Sweat is stinging your eyes, your quads are burning, and your mouth is as dry as the Sahara

Fig. 5.2. The formulas in this chapter will help you establish your target heart rate curve much more accurately than by using the generalized target zone chart seen in many gyms and fitness studios.

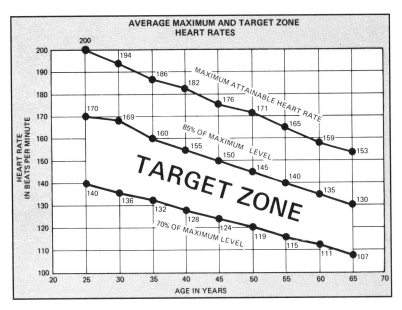

Desert. You reach for your neck, attempting to gauge your rapidly thumping pulse. Good luck.

Here's another illustration depicting the obstacles cyclists must overcome when taking their heart rates manually. Imagine doing intervals in early November with the mercury hovering around 40°F (4°C). After each 100 meter dash, you feather the brakes and sit up. You pull off one of your thermal gloves and place a finger inside your jacket collar and under that turtleneck. Several more seconds pass before you finally locate the carotid artery. Again, you will need a lot of good fortune to obtain an accurate pulse reading. On account of the multiplier used, if you happen to add or miss just one or two heart beats while counting, you can end up with a plus or minus of 20 bpm.

Case History: Jack's Fatigue

Jack, a 38-year old businessman, had been riding his bike for 4 years to stay in shape. He began finding it impossible to train more than four days a week without taking a day or two off due to fatigue. Also, during the evenings after a ride, he would fall asleep early and have difficulty getting out of bed the next morning.

When Jack began working out with an HRM, he immediately disovered that his pulse rose above 170 bpm when climbing hills. This reading, as a consequence of his age, indicated he was definitely in an anaerobic state.

By using an HRM on all of his rides, Jack learned to climb hills at a pace dictated by his body. After about 2 weeks of training in the target zone, his pace on the hills began increasing, his energy returned, and he no longer felt compelled to go to bed early.

Need further proof of the limits of manual pulse-taking? Clinical research is available: Both recreational and world-class cyclists and triathletes were asked to wear HRMs during their prescribed workouts. When comparing simultaneously measured heart rates taken by hand with those registered on the monitors, the former readings were consistently lower.

Relating Heart Rate to Performance

Some well-heeled athletes who want to fine-tune their training and uncover secrets about their bodies' limits spend quite a bit of time and money at sports physiology laboratories. There, health professionals put them through a rigorous battery of tests. This research provides the athlete with a knowledge about his or her blood lactate and muscle lactic acid levels, maximum oxygen uptake, respiratory quotient, and heart rate. The last two factors are particularly valuable.

Respiratory quotient indicates how the body is utilizing oxygen and carbon dioxide. Through this assessment, it can be ascertained whether an athlete is primarily burning fat or sugar while exercising. This procedure is performed by measuring the amount of oxygen the body consumes and comparing it to the quantity of carbon dioxide exhaled. The mathematical ratio of carbon dioxide to oxygen is called RQ (Respiratory Quotient), R Value, or RER (Respiratory Exchange Rate). It ranges from 0.7 to 1.0. As an athlete's R Value gets closer to 0.7, it denotes that more fat is being used to fuel the body. When the value tilts closer to 1.0, this suggests that sugar, in increasing amounts, is the dominant energy source.

The second factor—heart rate—can be used alone to conduct all the previously mentioned research that a sports lab performs, because the heart rate accurately parallels these other factors. In effect, you have an inexpensive and practical method for evaluating your physical condition as well as the effectiveness of your workouts right at your fingertips.

This was not always the case, though. Up until the early 1980s, there were only two heart rate evaluation procedures available: the *talk test*—which originated with the 1970s running craze—and a quasi-scientific formula based on an athlete's chronological age. The talk test assumes that you are exercising within the aerobic range if you can comfortably talk to your training partner during a workout. This test, however, is about as reliable as the flip of a coin, since the chances are 50–50 you will be either right or wrong.

Given these odds, the quasi-scientific method seems infinitely more reliable for structuring a training program based on the athlete's heart rate. This system, which is still widely used today, instructs riders to subtract their age from 220 and multiply the difference by a figure ranging from 65 to 85 percent. Supposedly, the resulting number provides the athlete with the maximum heart beats per minute (bpm) for keeping workouts aerobic—or, rather, just at the *anaerobic threshold* (AT).

Table 5.1. Relationship of heart rate, blood lactate, maximum oxygen uptake, and expired air

Treadmill Speed (km/h)	Rest	10	12	14	16	18
HR (bpm)	75	141	153	166	179	192
Lactate (mmol/l)	1.30	1.75	1.87	2.72	4.83	11.1
$VO_{2\,max}$ (ml/min)	323	2617	3017	3494	3960	4465
VE (l/min)	13.6	67.1	79.5	96.4	119.3	151.0

Data from: Kindermann et al. *European Journal of Applied Physiology,* 42: 25–34, 1979.

Technically, exercising at AT means you have reached the highest level of oxygen uptake, or the point at which, regardless of the workload, you can't consume any more oxygen. Yet, the term *threshold*, as defined in the AT method, refers to the onset of anaerobic exercise. This approach to training, therefore, emphasizes anaerobic efforts—however mild they may be—as opposed to aerobic activities.

The assumed rationale for this approach contains two fallacies. First, it assumes that 220 minus age will render an athlete's maximum heart rate. But if you are to derive conditioning benefits by means of this equation you must push yourself to the max—otherwise the formula simply isn't valid. Second, the multiplier (65%–85%) is an arbitrary figure that doesn't consider an athlete's overall health and fitness.

Before dismissing this method, it's essential to examine the concept of AT training. The leading proponent of this practice is the Italian physiologist Dr. Francesco Conconi. He was among the first in the sports medicine profession to bring his laboratory out on the road in order to work with cyclists. Conconi's pioneering efforts received widespread attention on January 23, 1984, thanks to the astounding achievement of the then 32-year-old Italian racer Francesco Moser. Moser, who was trained by Conconi, established a new hour speed record for the bicycle—51.151 km. Moser's accomplishment, especially in light of his age, sold the cycling community on AT training.

Indeed, Conconi's AT concept was a real breakthrough as a way of training cyclists and other athletes.* In fact, some of the procedures outlined in this book parallel his work. The

---

* Because the physiological basis of AT training is extremely complex, those desiring more detailed information on this subject should consult the study "Determination of the Anaerobic Threshold by a Noninvasive Field Test in Runners," by Conconi et al, published by the American Physiological Society in 1982.

major differences between the information presented here and that offered by Conconi are in the realms of philosophy and physiology, as well as in experience.

Conconi believes the ideal training level is achieved by exercising at your AT. *The High Performance Heart*, by contrast, takes the position that Maximum Aerobic Function (MAF)— the heart rate that produces the most aerobic benefits with the least anaerobic stimulation—is the optimal method of obtaining fitness. That's because, as previously mentioned, the conditioning effect on your aerobic system is inhibited when you become even slightly anaerobic.

Athletes who utilize the MAF conditioning concept, as opposed to AT training, can be assured of several positive results: They will not only develop their aerobic system, but they will also perform anaerobic workouts, which are mandatory for competitive events. By combining these two exercise patterns, you can promote fitness without risking your good health.

Since your overall well-being is on the line, you need an accurate method to determine your heart rate. In a medical setting, ascertaining the exact relationship between heart rate and aerobic state is achieved by clinically establishing an athlete's true, or physiological, age. Different doctors do this in different ways. What they commonly evaluate, however, are the lungs' vital capacity, the blood sugar level, and the condition of the heart (by using an electrocardiogram), as well as an individual's personal and family history.

What becomes readily apparent from such medical analysis is that a 40-year-old athlete may have the body efficiency (the ability to perform an athletic task) of an individual either 10 years older or 20 years younger. (Francesco Moser clearly falls into the latter category: In January 1994, at age 42, he bettered his own previous best and former world record by covering 51.840 km in an hour.) As a consequence of physiological condition, the true age of a 40-year-old athlete may be closer to 50 or 20, respectively.

Doctors can help athletes establish their correct heart rate. Yet it is quite possible to make this determination on your own with reasonable accuracy. All you have to do is to follow this easy 2-step formula:

Step 1:
Subtract your chronological age from 180.

Step 2:
Place yourself in one of the four categories below and adjust the number derived in Step 1 accordingly:

Category A
If you have never trained before, are recovering from a major

---

Case History: Susan's Injuries

Susan, 29, was a cycling veteran of 10 years whose specialty was century rides. Still, she was continually plagued by injuries. When asked if she had ever ridden with an HRM, Susan replied, "Oh, I use one all the time." What she didn't use, however, was the proper formula to determine her target zone's parameters. Given Susan's age and the fact that she was experiencing health problems, her maximum training heart rate should have been around 146 bpm. Instead, she had calculated her top end at 155 bpm, believing that cycling experience was the most important factor.

Upon correctly using the 180 formula, Susan resumed her long-distance cycling regimen—and was no longer beset by the persistent injuries.

injury, operation, or illness, or are taking medication, subtract 10 from the number obtained in Step 1.

Category B

If you are currently exercising, but have been falling short of your goals (e.g., improved fitness, better competitive results, more energy, weight loss, etc.), or your workout routine is inconsistent, or you have suffered an injury (even a minor one), or you have had more than 2 colds or cases of the flu during the past year, subtract 5 from the number obtained in Step 1.

Category C

If for the past year you have worked out consistently (4 or more times per week), have progressed to your satisfaction (feel fitter, enjoyed improved competitive results, have more energy, lost weight, etc.) and have not suffered any injury or experienced no more than 2 colds or cases of the flu, do not alter the number obtained in Step l.

Category D

If you compete, and your performance has improved over the past 2 years, you have not suffered any injuries or experienced more than 2 colds or cases of the flu during the past year, then add 5 to the number obtained in Step 1.

More than likely, you will easily be able to find a suitable category and obtain a specific numerical value. This figure, regardless of the category, is the maximum heart rate that will keep you aerobic when training.

"In Between" Status

Some athletes, however, may be in a quandary over how to determine their exact maximum heart rate figure. Due to a

variety of circumstances, they feel as though they fall in between categories. If you are in this situation, just select the
more conservative number.

Here is a typical example of an athlete who qualifies for "in
between" status. He is 35 years old and has been working out
for 3 years—despite experiencing a nagging injury (e.g., a
minor knee problem or lower back pain). If your situation is
similar, no matter how old you are, compute your maximum
heart rate in this manner:

Step 1:
180 minus age
$180 - 35 = 145$

Step 2:
Choose category B and subtract 5:
$145 - 5 = 140$

In this case, your maximum heart rate would be 140 bpm.
Generally, the figure derived this way will enable training
without harming the body and still provide fat-burning, aerobic benefits. Should your heart rate exceed 140 bpm, however, you would not only start burning more sugar and less
fat, but also risk the possibility of aggravating the injury.

Upon arriving at a number that indicates your peak heart
rate, you should establish a *bpm range*. The most serviceable
span is 10 bpm below your top end, since it's often difficult to
keep your heart rate at its designated maximum. If your
maximum aerobic heart rate is 165 bpm, for example, you will
still derive conditioning and health gains at your low end of
155 bpm.

All of this, perhaps, prompts the question of how the 180
formula was derived. Simply put, through trial and error.
During the early 1980s, doctors in laboratories saw the obvious and effective relationship between lower RQ (fat burn-

ing) and a specified heart rate. They called this figure the maximum heart rate. At this point, I decided to come up with an accurate and accessible heart rate formula, since it was financially impractical for most people to go to a sports physiology laboratory.

Starting in 1982, I began correlating the RQs and heart rates of hundreds of athletes. By carefully studying elite performers as well as casual exercisers, I made a very important dicovery: Relatively lower training heart rates, based on the 180 formula, ultimately provided these athletes with more aerobic function—and endurance. Still, while the 180 figure is an arbitrary one, it does not attempt to establish an athlete's maximum heart rate, as the 220 formula does, by deducting the athlete's chronological age.

Because the 180 formula takes into account an athlete's health as well as his or her fitness, it will be more precise than its 220 counterpart. The 4 categories, however, are similar in

Fig. 5.3. Co-author Dr. Philip Maffetone (right) and ultra-marathon champion Stu Mittleman examine Respiratory Quotient data on the computer.

rationale to the 65%–85% multipliers used in the 220 formula. Even in this area, the 180 method has demonstrated greater reliability.

For over a decade, the 180 system has been used to clinically monitor the heart rates of athletes whose abilities ranged from novice to superstar. Moreover, during this same period, the 4-category plan has proven to be much more reliable than the percentage multiplier approach as a means of establishing an individual athlete's maximum heart rate. And even more significant is the fact that when compared with laboratory tests, the 180 equation correlated amazingly well.

However, while the 180 formula can confirm your correct target zone, it does not guarantee your overall well-being. To reach a state where health and fitness are equally balanced, you must have a reliable means of recording your heart rate, and this is where the heart rate monitor comes in.

Chapter 6

Evaluating Heart Rate Monitors

If you want hassle-free, accurate heart rate information, you should rely on a heart rate monitor. Currently, there are three types of HRMs available on the market: the wired digital pulse-point unit, the wired, and the wireless chest wall devices. Each of these comes in a wide variety of models. (A fourth type may be launched soon, as described in the section *HRM of the Future?* at the end of this chapter.)

Fig. 6.1. The heart rate monitor should always be worn directly around the chest wall cavity and never over clothing. Use water to moisten the electrode strap to improve contact with the skin. Since perspiration buildup hampers accurate recording of the heart rate, the strap should be periodically cleaned in a mild soapy water solution.

The pulse-point unit, operating on the principle of photo-reflectance, depends on a photo-cell and a light source to record your heart rate. A sensor equipped with a surgical rubber gripper is fastened to either the fingertip or earlobe. The passage of blood through the vessels in either extremity blocks out the light with each pulse beat. The receiver's timer circuitry, which can be clipped onto a runner's singlet or a cyclist's jersey, converts this information into a displayed heart rate.

The primary virtue of a pulse-point HRM is price. It can be purchased for between $25 to $50. But bear in mind that you get just what you pay for. Indeed, the technological limitations of a pulse-point monitor are considerable. While this type of HRM is acceptable for indoor use, it doesn't work well outdoors where the light source is inconsistent. Also, usually the unit doesn't allow you to program the upper and lower reaches of your target zone. Consequently, cyclists will frequently have to take their eyes off the road—certainly not a

Fig. 6.2. Early HRMs, still used on stationary bikes, have sensors that are clipped to the earlobe. However, at higher than moderate heart rates, these units become less accurate due to distortions of the pulses in the ear lobe. (photo courtesy Cat Eye)

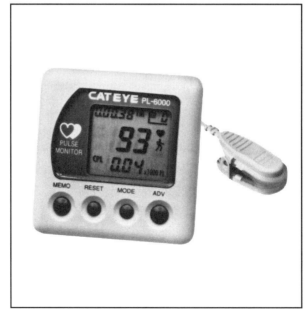

safe practice—to see their heart rate on the receiver. Further-more, this device is extremely sensitive to body movements, so its accuracy becomes questionable during intense exertion—such as when thrusting a bike from side to side during a demanding hill climb. Despite these constraints, the pulse-point device is definitely more accurate than manual pulse taking or the talk test. Still, this type of HRM will prove unsatisfactory if you are seriously concerned about fitness or competition.

In order to get the most out of your workouts, at least invest in a wired chest wall HRM. This instrument is much more accurate than its pulse-point counterpart, because it reads the heart's electrical activity. These electrical impulses, which are transmitted through the skin, are picked up by a comfortable, lightweight chest belt equipped with rubber-covered sensors. The heart rate data are transmitted by a wire (which can be routed through the sleeve of your jersey) to the wristwatch-like receiver. If you choose to mount the receiver on the

Fig. 6.3. The Polar Accurex II heart rate monitor is water resistant and includes functions such as target zone monitoring signals, stopwatch, and a memory to recall critical information afterward. (photo courtesy Polar)

handlebars, the wire can be run out the jersey's bottom or collar and secured to the frame's top tube.

The more sophisticated units offer a feature that is essential for all athletes, regardless of their exercise regimen: audible upper and lower alarm signal settings that can be precisely pre-programmed to the target zone. When you hear the alarm beeping, you know it's time to increase or decrease your effort.

The wired HRM has some drawbacks, however. The cable joining the chest belt's sensors to the receiver can restrict your movements, and it may be inadvertently disconnected or become entangled—which could cause a severe accident on a bicycle. These disconcerting qualities notwithstanding, expect to pay between $100–$175 for this type of unit.

The best all-around HRM is the wireless chest wall telemetry instrument. It relies on radio waves to transmit your heart information from the chest strap sensors to its wristwatch-like receiver. Like the wired unit, the telemetric monitor has clock and stopwatch functions, as well as pre-programmable alarms to signal that you are exercising above or below the target zone. Like its cable correlate, the receiver can be mounted on a bike's handlebars. These features enable you to keep your eyes on the road, since you can either hear or momentarily glance at your heart rate. Furthermore, because a telemetric HRM operates without wires, there's nothing to become entangled, disconnected, or to restrict your body's movements.

Other available options on some of these monitors include the ability to record the amount of time you have spent in the target zone, the displaying and cataloguing of split times, and the availability of cadence and altimeter functions. And swimmers will appreciate that some models are waterproof.

The top-of-the-line model has the capacity to store up to 8 hours of exercise statistics for as many as 15 races or workout sessions. Moreover, this performance information can be downloaded to a personal computer. The interface package contains the necessary software to enable you to make an in-depth analysis of your heart rate data.

Because telemetric HRMs are precise and versatile, they are also very costly. Depending on the model you select, be prepared to fork out anywhere from $125 to $430.

Regardless of the HRM you choose—pulse-point, wired or wireless chest wall—your money will be well spent, because next to your bike, swimming suit or running shoes, it will be your most important piece of training equipment. Consider this: The heart rate monitor essentially provides you with the equivalent of a personal coach who gives you immediate feedback. And because the HRM is accurate and objective, it

Fig. 6.4. The Polar Optimex is for use on a stationary bike. The transmitter is worn around the chest and the receiver is mounted on the bike. It provides information about your high and low aerobic ranges, measures total elapsed time and stores information on exercise time spent in the target zone. (photo courtesy Polar)

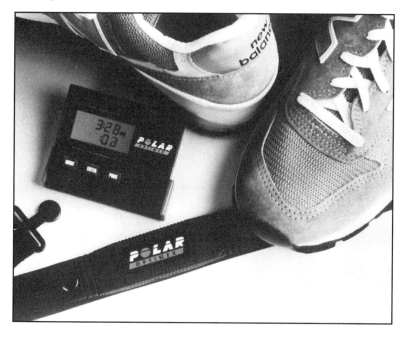

can effectively help you meet your goals for fitness or competition.

HRM of the Future?

Heart rate monitor technology has fundamentally remained the same for the past 15 years. In the mid-80s, however, manufacturers altered the unit's physical appearance to make it more user-friendly.

Initially, the chest strap transmitter was attached to a wide strip of cloth. By means of a wire, it sent the heart rate signal to a bulky receiver fastened to the athlete's waist, or a bicycle's handlebars. The next generation of monitors featured a smaller chest strap, and transmitted the heart rate—without wire—to a receiver placed in a wristwatch.

Fig. 6.5. With a computer, you can plot out your progress for a truly scientific approach to training. With the appropriate hardware and software, you can keep track of your workouts. Examples of such graphs are shown in Chapter 7.

The upside of these new wireless monitors is that they are comfortable, convenient, and, in some instances, waterproof. On the downside, there is some loss of accuracy along with the risk of transmission interference. For example, riding or running in a group with other monitor users often find athletes picking up one anothers' heart rate! That can happen because the analog receiver doesn't distinguish which signal it's getting. This all too common problem plagues people working out in aerobic classes, also. Besides this annoyance, exercisers on stationary electronic mechanisms—like computerized bikes, stair climbers, and treadmills—can experience fluctuations in their heart rate displays because these machines send out an electromagnetic field.

But help could be on the way fairly soon, thanks to the efforts of Dr. Terry Gorman, a chiropractor. Unlike the analog signal that most heart rate monitors currently rely on, Gorman has invented a device that utilizes a digital transmitting system. Basically, this

Fig. 6.6. The Sensor Dynamics Cross Trainer is water resistant. It monitors heart rate, current and average speed, trip distance, real time, and elapsed time (courtesy Sensor Dynamics)

means the heart rate is sent from the chest strap to the wrist-watch receiver on its own radio channel.

How and why does Gorman do that? His Mohapac, New York, company, Aerobic Tools, has an FCC-approved radio frequency which allows for the transmitting of heart rate data. This enables Gorman to assign an identification number to each heart rate signal, which permits athletes wearing his monitors to train together—without the hassle of inaccurate pulse measurements.

Should the transmission signal be affected by an electro-magnetic field, however, the receiver will reject the heart rate number. And if the watch is unable to obtain an accurate pulse readout for more than 21 seconds, it shuts down automatically. Gorman feels these attributes will make his heart rate monitor "the most reliable one on the planet." Perhaps so, but it won't come with any of the features—target zone alarms, stopwatch, clock—that are standard on most of these gadgets. Expect to pay $100 for this digital device when it debuts during the fall of 1994.

Chapter 7

Warming Up and Cooling Down: Keys to Health and Fitness

When asked to explain their warmup and cool-down routines, many athletes express anything from bewilderment to disdain. Others, who do take the time to perform these tasks, assume a very casual attitude. As for warming up, they say they spend a few minutes taking it easy before going all out. And their cool-down period concludes the moment they have

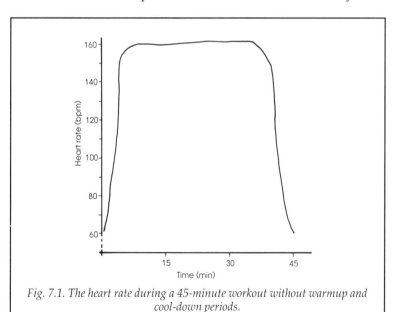

Fig. 7.1. The heart rate during a 45-minute workout without warmup and cool-down periods.

caught their breath. If any of these responses reflect your opening and closing exercise patterns, you are a candidate for health and/or fitness problems.

Warming up and cooling down are the two most essential elements of any training program. Neglecting the former practice can cause overuse injuries, while ignoring the latter can diminish the gains derived from exercising. In terms of heart rate, this is the situation illustrated in Fig. 7.1.

The Warmup

When your body is at rest, most of the blood is circulating through the organs and glands—such as the adrenal and thyroid, the liver, kidneys, and pancreas—as well as other primary areas—like the nerves, brain, heart and intestines. How you treat these organs and glands at the onset and at the

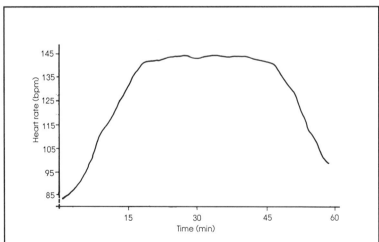

Fig. 7.2. The heart rate during a 60-minute workout with warmup and cool-down periods. During the warmup, the heart rate slowly rises to the maximum training level after about 15 minutes. The cool-down begins about 15 minutes before the end of the workout. During this period, the heart rate is slowly lowered, ending just above the starting heart rate.

conclusion of a workout effects not only your conditioning but also your overall health.

As you start your workout, your heart rate naturally increases, and more blood is shunted to the muscles engaged in the activity. As with any other sudden dramatic change to your body, the rapid redistribution of blood—away from the organs and glands, to the active muscles—can be very stressful. To ensure that you don't incur any physical damage, this blood redistribution process, or shunting, should occur very gradually. This gradual shunting of blood away from the organs and glands into the working muscles is the definition—as well as the purpose—of warming up.

Case History: Jonathan's Tension

When cycling, 48-year old Jonathan took extreme care to keep his heart rate within the correct target zone. Since his body was often tight upon getting out of bed, he wisely spent at least 15 minutes warming up on early morning training rides. But Jonathan had a hectic daily schedule crammed with family, business, and social responsibilities. Therefore, to save a few minutes, he would come racing into his driveway at the end of a ride.

Sometimes, within an hour after a workout, his muscles would cramp and stiffen up. When this happened, he gobbled down two aspirin to ease the stress on his body. "I just don't have the time," Jonathan said, after being told he needed to spend 15 minutes cooling down. Yet he agreed to follow this procedure for one week, and was amazed that such a seemingly little thing could make such a big difference in how he felt. Free of the post-ride aspirin, Jonathan feels good all day, and his morning tightness has begun to dissipate.

A warmup period at a low output level (i.e., using low gears in the case of cycling, a slow pace for runners and swimmers) for 10 to 15 minutes will allow your heart rate to rise gradually and prepare the body for the demands of exercising. The HRM plays a crucial role in this procedure. It keeps you aware of your pulse figures and their relationship to the shunting factor.

Figure 7.2 illustrates a proper warmup with regard to heart rate and time for a one-hour aerobic workout, for an athlete whose maximum pulse is 145 bpm. In this example, the first 12 minutes are devoted to warming up. At the end of this period, the heart rate should be in the target zone. Should a workout exceed 1½ hours, then the warmup time should be extended to 20 minutes.

Figure 7.3 shows how an athlete who will be working out for 2 hours gradually and safely brings the heart rate into the target zone.

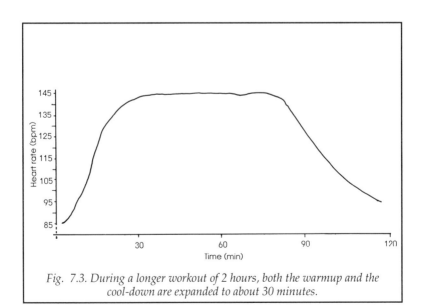

Fig. 7.3. During a longer workout of 2 hours, both the warmup and the cool-down are expanded to about 30 minutes.

The Cool-Down

Equally as significant as preparing your body for rigorous activity is giving it fair warning that the workout is ending. This is the cool-down period. If you don't take the time to perform this task correctly, too much blood tends to remain, or pool, in the muscles. When pooling occurs, the normal circulation of blood is impeded.

During the cool-down, the blood is gradually recirculated back to the organs and glands. In the immediate post-exercise phase, blood is used for oxygen and nutrients necessary to repair the cells that were engaged during training or competition. The removal of waste generated during activity, such as cellular debris and carbon dioxide, is also dependent upon good circulation. Consequently, if you don't take the time to cool down adequately, blood pools in the muscles and reduces some of the health benefits of exercising.

The duration of the cool-down segment should correspond proportionally to the time you have been working out.

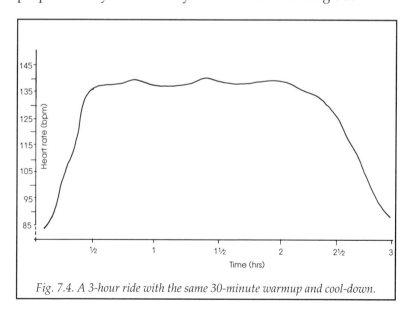

Fig. 7.4. A 3-hour ride with the same 30-minute warmup and cool-down.

Figure 7.4 illustrates an athlete involved in a 3-hour practice session. This person's maximum pulse is 165 bpm. Twenty to 30 minutes are spent warming up, and 20 to 30 minutes will be spent cooling down.

Some Special—and not so Special—Circumstances

Let's assume you are pressed for time and can only exercise for half an hour, or that you're a novice and this is the extent of your training program. In either one of these instances, you will spend most of your exercise time just warming up and cooling down. And even when this is the length of your training session, you can still accumulate fitness assets.

Figure 7.5 illustrates an athlete whose pulse should not exceed 135 bpm, exercising for 30 minutes. In this case, the warmup and the cool-down periods are 15 minutes each.

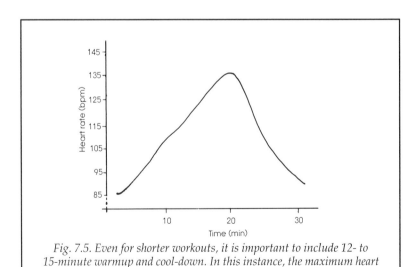

Fig. 7.5. Even for shorter workouts, it is important to include 12- to 15-minute warmup and cool-down. In this instance, the maximum heart rate is not maintained for long at all. This workout is mostly warming up and cooling down, but still provides many health benefits.

More than likely, this illustration provokes the question: How can only warming up and cooling down provide any fitness or health benefits? Exercise can be defined in numerous ways. One definition is that it is the increase in the body's metabolism, or metabolic rate, beyond a resting state. What is really significant, then, is how much time is required to make this transition.

Most athletes, whether they are fit or out of shape, can make this shift in about 12 minutes. Consequently, they not only have enough time to warm up and cool down, but also briefly work in the target zone. An individual who regularly spends 10 or more hours per week exercising should not scoff at the value of occasional 30-minute sessions. Indeed, over the long haul, these short journeys will definitely be a boon to both health and conditioning.

Figure 7.6 represents an athlete training for 45 minutes. Observe that the only major difference between this and the previous example is the amount of time—15 minutes—spent maintaining the maximum heart rate of 135 bpm.

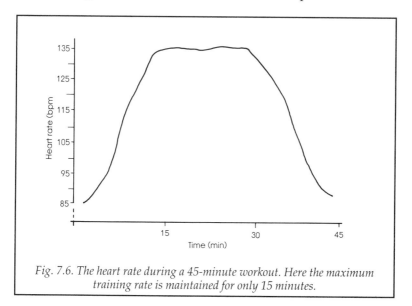

Fig. 7.6. The heart rate during a 45-minute workout. Here the maximum training rate is maintained for only 15 minutes.

Since people in general, and athletes in particular, tend to compare themselves with one another, note this well: The heart rates of two athletes can be radically different, even when they are both performing at the same output level. This can happen due to the differences in individuals' unique physical ability and body chemistry. So, even if you are a cyclist who can keep up with 3-time Tour de France winner Greg LeMond, don't expect to have the same heart rate as he does.

Ultimately, the best reason to warm up and cool down adequately is that both of these tasks can greatly reduce your chances of sustaining an injury. Studies show that athletes who don't engage in these routines are more prone to physical problems than those who scrupulously perform these activities.

For both the casual exerciser and the world-class athlete, an HRM removes the guesswork from the warming up and cooling down periods. Don't dismiss the value of these pre- and post-workout functions just because you're not pushing your body to its maximum. Take the time to get up to and down from speed gradually. This will ensure that you get the most out of your training program.

Chapter 8

Training With the Heart Rate Monitor

Most athletes—especially those interested in competition—can benefit from a yearly training program. Each day can be put to good use, whether it's devoted to working out, racing, recovering, or simply maintaining your equipment. But even if you're not interested in competition, a 12-month training schedule is still very valuable. Besides giving your workouts a daily, as well as a long-range focus, it enables you to follow two critical rules while exercising:

Rule Number 1:

All of your aerobic workouts should be performed in the target zone. Even though your emphasis is on Maximum Aerobic Function, it's quite possible to become "too aerobic." In order to maintain a balance in your physical conditioning, there are times throughout the year that you must engage in anaerobic activities. Using an HRM for this type of exercise—whether it be sprints, intervals, or racing—is very important, since it allows you to safely push your body to the prescribed threshold.

Rule Number 2:

In order to objectively evaluate your physical conditioning, it is necessary to establish several performance benchmarks. By doing this, you can regularly note any changes in fitness. For example, by comparing the time it takes to ride the same 10-mile loop in the target zone on a weekly basis, you will obtain concrete knowledge as to whether or not you're making fitness advances. Furthermore, at the conclusion of every workout, you should become aware of another crucial conditioning reference point—recovery time, or how long it takes the heart rate to return to "normal" after the stress of exercising.

Athletes intent on improving their health and fitness must adhere to these fundamental training axioms. And due to its aforementioned virtues, an HRM is an indispensable tool for maintaining these exercise principles.

Before designing your yearly training program, it's advisable to take 6 factors into consideration:

Fig. 8.1 (this page) and Fig. 8.2 (opposite page). In addition to developing line graphs of your workouts, the computerized heart rate programs allow you to shift to bar charts (below) and numerical charts (facing page). The program also has a built-in Conconi calculation to determine your anaerobic threshold.

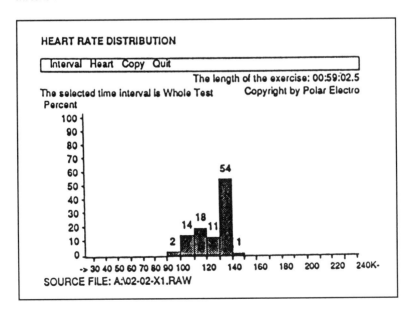

HEART RATE DISTRIBUTION

Interval Heart Copy Quit

The length of the exercise: 00:59:02.5

The selected time interval is Whole Test   Copyright by Polar Electro

Percent

SOURCE FILE: A:\02-02-X1.RAW

1. Scheduling:

Very few of us are going to become world-class athletes. Keeping this in mind, be realistic when creating your exercise calendar. Make sure you leave enough time to fulfill your responsibilities to family and friends, comfortably meet your work and/or education commitments, and still have the opportunity for leisure activities. By taking all of these factors into account, you will have a better chance of sticking to your training schedule and, therefore, successfully integrating exercise into your lifestyle.

2. Physical Condition:

Ask yourself this basic question: Am I able to withstand the stress of daily exercising? If you have any uncertainty about your response, see a sports doctor and get a thorough physical checkup.

3. Biochemical Issues:

Because you are about to make some considerable demands on your body, it's important to provide it with the proper

HEART RATE LISTING

NextPage	PreviousPage	Hardcopy	Interm.	Next	Quit

Copyright by POLAR ELECTRO   SOURCE FILE: Noname

Time   Heart Rate Values

Time											
00:00	78	77	76	73	73	74	77	81	82	78	74	74
00:01	76	76	76	75	78	76	75	75	75	76	77	76
00:02	77	77	78	80	87	88	81	76	72	75	77	75
00:03	75	75	79	80	77	82	79	73	74	75	76	73
00:04	70	73	77	81	79	80	79	78	74	77	75	73
00:05	71	69	70	72	72	75	75	81	78	75	73	73
00:06	71	72	75	74	77	77	73	75	75	78	80	77
00:07	77	73	73	71	71	68	71	77	73	79	83	83
00:08	82	84	83	81	78	0	77	69	71	74	74	72
00:09	73	78	75	72	74	79	75	75	76	75	73	68

Final Time: 00.05.28

Intermediate Times:

HR 103   HR 166   HR 113
00.01.48,6   00.38.39,7   00.05.26,5

HR 170   HR 179
00.26.02,3   00.41.25,2

nutrients. Although this subject clearly does not fall within the scope of the present book, you should be aware of it and make sure your diet is well balanced.

4. Psychological Issues:

Studies have shown that when people exercise in the morning, as opposed to the evening, they have a greater chance of staying with a regular training program. Whether you choose to train in the morning or the afternoon, adhere to a consistent schedule. Knowing *when* you are supposed to ride will encourage the maintenance of your routine. (All of this is not to say that some athletes don't possess the discipline to train at different times on different days, should they want to.)

For the purpose of organization, self-analysis, and motivation, keep a training diary. Each day, enter the following data: your morning pulse—which should be taken before getting out of bed—how long you remained in the target during your workout, and a few words about what you did, or did not, accomplish.

Regardless of whether you are exercising for fitness or competition, be realistic about the goals you are setting. Unless you are extremely talented, don't expect to establish any long-distance records or win a lot of races during your first year of training or competition. Some people who set unrealistic goals become discouraged and give up if they find out they can't fulfill their unrealistic expectations. That's the last thing you want to happen.

Tailor your goals to your age and ability. In the case of cycling, some reasonable objectives may include riding continuously for one hour, completing a 50-mile ride, or finishing with the pack during a race. No matter where you're positioned on the exercise spectrum, there is a value to reflecting on your goals and developing the correct strategy to meet them.

5. Habit Changes:

Sedentary individuals choosing to launch a training program are, first of all, changing their habits. And altering a deep-seated disposition is extremely difficult. For some people, just allotting time in the day to exercise can be a more formidable task than the workout itself.

When you begin a workout regimen, you may be cultivating a new mind-set; consequently it may be useful to adopt the notion that you are in the process of creating a positive addiction. In effect, you will be repeating an activity on a daily basis that will both nourish and excite your mind and body. How long it takes to develop this exercise pattern, and its associated responses, depends on your degree of commitment.

Generally, many novice athletes see their commitment begin to waver at two very specific moments. Initially, they have trouble mustering the requisite energy that will take them

Fig. 8.3. Heart rate monitor software will plot your workout with great accuracy. This 40 km time trial shows a fairly consistent racing heart rate throughout.

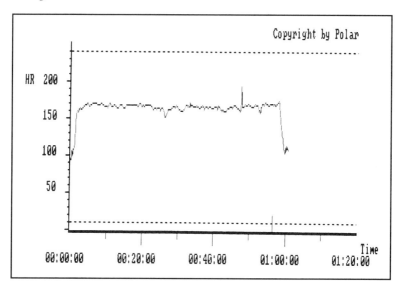

from the easy chair to their bicycle or other exercise equipment. Once they have surmounted that obstacle, they face another rough spot: At some point during the first month of training, they will experience a loss of enthusiasm.

Being aware of such snares has some value. However, an effective way of avoiding both of these unsettling circumstances is to make plans to join forces with people who have already established a training routine. If you opt for this kind of psychological support from experienced friends, don't make the mistake of trying to keep pace with them. This could prove extremely discouraging. Instead, go at your own speed and make plans to meet them at designated points.

6. Time:

For both novice and seasoned athletes, most workouts should be based on time, rather than on miles or laps. Time is a qualitative factor. And the body responds much better to the stress of time than the stress of distance, which is decidedly quantitative.

With regard to time, neophytes would profit from adopting the attitude that less is more. Why? Short exercise sessions reduce your chances of sustaining an injury, help keep your enthusiasm at a high level, and, most important, foster the exercise habit. Given all of these factors, those who are just beginning an exercise regimen should not work out any longer than 30 minutes per session during the first 2 to 3 months of their program.

However, certainly in the case of cycling, extended workout periods, as well as longer distances, do assume significance for experienced athletes. Both of these elements have to be taken into consideration, for example, when performing long, steady rides, speed work, and intervals. In such instances, numbers (miles, time, and heart rate) allow cyclists to adapt their training program to how they feel (rested or tired) and prepare for competition.

After you have taken all of these 6 factors into consideration, you are ready to formulate a personal yearly training program. A sample is listed below for a cyclist, while this regimen can be adapted easily for other athletic pursuits as well.

Yearly Training Program for Competitive and Noncompetitive Cyclists

☐ November 15 to December 1: Rest Period

☐ December 1 to April 1: Aerobic Base and Cross-Training

☐ April 1 to July 1: Incorporate Anaerobic Training and Racing

☐ July 1 to August 15: Aerobic Base and Break from Racing

☐ August 15 to November 15: Incorporate Anaerobic Training and Racing

This 365-day schedule allows both competitive and noncompetitive athletes ample time to develop their aerobic and anaerobic systems. The program's key feature, which will enable you to reach this two-fold objective, is, in a word, *specificity*. This means that at various times of the year, you will be working on particular aspects of your health and conditioning. In order to truly harmonize both of these dimensions, it is crucial to be ruthlessly objective. And when it comes to presenting impartial, precise information about your body, there's no better device than an HRM.

Rest Period (November 15 to December 1)

Most likely, you will welcome the onset of these two weeks. It's free time to do whatever you like. And, most importantly, the rest reriod provides a psychological break from your workout regimen. But just because you are on a vacation from training doesn't mean you should overeat, drink to excess, and totally ignore your body. Use these two weeks wisely: Besides resting and relaxing, take some fun rides or participate in some nondemanding sports activity. To do otherwise may cause you to pay the piper during the next phase of your training program.

Fig. 8.4. When viewed after training, certain inconsistencies, such as the cadence in this 2 hr, 15 min workout, become apparent.

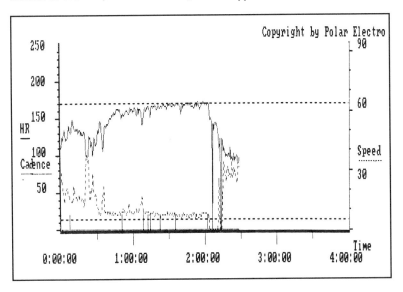

Aerobic Base and Cross-Training (December 1 to April 1)

Having rejuvenated your mind and body, you're probably more than ready to begin training in earnest. Your reintroduction to serious exercise begins with developing your aerobic base. Put simply, this is the period of time in the yearly training plan when you should engage only in aerobic activity. Consequently, you will not perform any anaerobic workouts—and that means not competing in other sports disciplines, such as track and cyclocross races, cross-country skiing, swimming, and running competitions, etc., unless, of course, you can remain in the aerobic range.

Rebuilding the aerobic system correctly requires several months of abstaining from anaerobic activity. That's because anaerobic exercise can interfere with aerobic progress, or your ability to do more work at any given heart rate.

Depending on the individual and his or her level of fitness, anaerobic workouts can produce varied consequences. For the extremely fit and healthy person, these intense efforts will usually cause only a mild disruption of aerobic progress. On the other hand, if you are not in great shape, or have been ill and/or injured, anaerobic workouts can bring about major training setbacks: You will either endure the termination of all aerobic benefits or experience an actual regression in aerobic fitness.

The reason why anaerobic activity can hinder aerobic functioning is not entirely clear. One known connection, however, is that lactic acid—which is increasingly produced during anaerobic activity—can interfere with the body's chemical functions that enable aerobic metabolism to take place.

To ensure that aerobic metabolism takes place without any impediments, most athletes would profit from biannual aerobic base periods. The longer rebuilding stage should begin in early December and last until mid-March, and a shorter term would start in early July and continue on into mid-August.

The time you will spend re-establishing your aerobic base is not written in stone. Typically, the first longer period lasts from 2 to 4 months. Some athletes, however, will require a greater or lesser duration to satisfy this essential fitness objective.

How long it takes to fully replenish the aerobic system depends on a variety of factors. If you have suffered bouts of illness or injuries, or have seen a steady decline in your performances, add 1 or 2 months to the regular aerobic base period. Conversely, if you are satisfied with both your race results and your level of fitness, and you have remained healthy, your aerobic base period may be as brief as 2 months.

Cross-Training

While you are in the process of revitalizing your aerobic system, take the opportunity to participate in some cross-training. One of the problems of becoming a single-sport specialist is that you may not realize your full body potential.

Many cyclists who are in reasonably good shape, for example, are unable to run up a long flight of stairs without gasping for breath. When racers, in particular, experience this situation, they usually exclaim something like, "I can't believe it! How could this happen?" Easy: It's the result of working out exclusively on their bicycles.

Generally, running—whether it's in the hills or on the flats —utilizes a set of muscle groups that the pedaling motion fails to develop. Moreover, when you sprint in sneakers, as opposed to sprinting on a bicycle, it makes different demands on your nervous system. And, if nothing else, cross-training's fundamental purpose is to educate your nervous system so that it can respond to a wide variety of exercises by stimulating the appropriate muscle fibers.

To reach this objective, cyclists can participate in any one of many activities during the aerobic base period. These include swimming, cross-country skiing, ice skating, rowing and even dancing and speed-walking. In many cases, cross-training may be a desirable alternative to cycling when the weather interferes with your activity on the bicycle.

Outdoor Riding in Cold Weather

If you live where the cold winds blow and the snow falls, it's imperative to take several precautions when riding outdoors. These warnings apply specifically to cycling, but to some extent may also be applicable when running.

Fig. 8.5. A steady heart rate is generally a sign of high efficiency during competition.

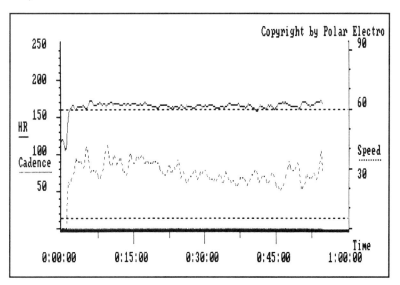

☐ When the temperature drops below 50° Farenheit (10°C), be sure to wear the proper clothing. Even though this may seem obvious, many cyclists still fall victim to frostbite injuries. The best way to ward off extremely cold weather is to dress in heat-conserving layers, topped off with wind-resistant thermals (jacket, tights, gloves, and booties). These garments are said to wick away moisture, but if you tend to sweat a lot, make sure the HRM is waterproof.

☐ Roads covered with snow and ice pose grave threats even to the most intrepid cyclists. Those riders driven to work out under these hazardous conditions should invest in a mountain bike. This low-to-the-ground machine, outfitted with road-gripping knobby tires, will give you a fighting chance to remain upright on slippery surfaces.

☐ Regardless of the bike you are riding or the clothes you are wearing, bear in mind that the windchill factor can be devastating, cooling your body much more than the air temperature may suggest.

☐ All your workouts require warmup and cool-down periods. In cold weather, avoid the unhealthy tendency to pedal faster at the onset of activity and to skip the cool-down period altogether. If the temperature is too low to perform these procedures, start and end your training session on a windload simulator.

Windload Simulator Training

Many cyclists who want to remain fit throughout the winter commonly rely on a windload simulator, or turbo-trainer. The equipment is a breeze to use. All that's required is slipping off the bike's front wheel (on some models even that is not neces-sary) and securing the fork into the trainer's quick-release assembly. The frame is mounted and clamped to the stand at its bottom bracket or held in place at the rear wheel axle. The rear wheel acts on a cylinder that drives wind turbines (or their inductive substitute). As you pedal and shift into higher gears, the resistance increases exponentially, similar to the wind resistance during outdoor cycling.

More often than not, cyclists become quite bored during windload simulator workouts. In an attempt to divert them-selves while getting nowhere fast, they read, watch television, or listen to music. Yet this task can be made entertaining and instructive, as well as more productive, simply by using a cyclocomputer (a device that measures speed, distance, ped-aling rate, etc.) and an HRM.

By observing these instruments while riding a windload simulator, you will probably notice some significant changes in your efforts. More than likely, you will be able to ride harder and faster in your prescribed target zone, as compared to cycling outdoors. Let's assume, for example, that your average road speed is 15 miles per hour while you're in the target zone. On a windload simulator, you may be able to simulate a riding speed that is 2 or 3 miles per hour faster—without any alter-ation in your normal heart rate.

To verify this observation, use a cyclocomputer in conjunction with your HRM. Once a week, either perform a 1-hour or a 25-mile time trial or administer the Maximum Aerobic Function examination. (See in the section *The MAF Test: Plotting the Data.*)

A windload simulator provides cyclists with an opportu-nity to perform out-of-the-saddle sprints and speed work, along with intervals. Limit all of these workout routines to 1¼ hours––to ride longer usually promotes boredom and a lack of enthusiasm for this task. And, of course, never omit your warmup and cool-down segments.

Roller Training

Rollers, unlike windload simulators, are not equipped with a bicycle support system. Upon placing your bike on the unit's three spinning drums, you have to balance it while you are pedaling, treadmill-fashion. Indeed, this approach to indoor training demands your complete attention. To do otherwise could send you tumbling into a piece of living room furniture.

Still, many cyclists are willing to take this inherent risk that comes with riding rollers. Along with keeping the cyclist focused, the apparatus definitely improves their form and pedaling technique, as well as their balance.

Adept roller riders can engage in the same indoor workouts as those who rely on windload simulators. Due to the tension associated with trying to remain vertical, however, they may not experience a similar drop in their target zone pulse.

The MAF Test: Plotting the Data

Sometime during the Aerobic Base Period, you will want to evaluate your fitness status. What guideline, then, is available to determine whether you are actually progressing or regressing, or on the verge of an injury or illness? The way to obtain all of this critical information is by measuring your Maximum Aerobic Function (MAF) with an HRM.

By comparing your heart rate with speed, distance, and time (if your HRM does not have the ability to record all of these data, it will be necessary to also employ a cyclocomputer), you will know exactly where you stand.

If you live in a cold climate, you can administer the MAF test while exercising indoors in winter. Then, when the weather becomes conducive to outdoor exercise, you will periodically do this test on your test course.

In cycling, the ideal place to conduct the MAF test is a velodrome. But since these banked, oval tracks are few and far between, you will probably have to find a substitute. The next best location is a stretch of open road, preferably a loop that can be ridden continuously—i.e., it must be free from traffic lights, stop signs and other obstacles that would force you to slow down or stop riding.

In this reasonably safe zone, you can determine your MAF. First warm up for 15 minutes, making sure your heart rate reaches its target zone. Having done this, ride your test course. Let's say that on your first effort you cover the circuit in 14 minutes. For the next 3 months, repeat the MAF test once a

Fig. 8.6 Andy Hampsten, a stage race specialist for the Motorola professional team, was one of the first racers to rely on the heart rate monitor.

week, making sure to record your times in your training diary after each effort.

If all goes well during these 12 weeks, you will probably build up your aerobic base. Your increasing fitness will be clearly indicated by the time reduction(s) on your test circuit.

One caveat: Time improvements in cycling are rarely constant or linear. Here's a typical bicycle scenario that exemplifies this phenomenon. Suppose after 3 months of consistent training, you have brought your test course time down from 14 to 12 minutes. Then, one day, you're suddenly jolted: It takes you 15 minutes to complete the circuit! Don't panic. There are several possible explanations for this apparent regression.

Often, the reason for a single increased test time is that you are simply having a bad day—and that even happens to top-echelon racers. A bad day can be attributed to several factors, some of which may be signaled by higher morning heart rates. For instance, you may have a cold or the flu coming on. Then, too, you may be experiencing excessive stress at home, work, or school. Still another possibility is that you could be a little burned out from overtraining.

Eventually, through self-analysis, you may be able to rectify some of these performance-detracting circumstances. Other factors, such as those listed below, however, will clearly be out of your control:

1. High humidity:
 cyclist will incur more riding resistance as the percentage of water in the air increases. As a result, it requires more effort to pedal a bike, which is evidenced by higher heart rates and increased MAF times.

2. Low Barometric Pressure:
When the barometric pressure is falling, it reduces the body's ability to take up oxygen. A quick check of your local

newspaper's weather map can tell you if this factor may be the reason for your weaker performance.

3. Wind resistance:
Cycling into a head wind requires a higher work output at the same speed, elevates the heart rate and can also lead to bio-chemical problems.

If your test course times either plateau or improve only slightly, there is nothing to worry about. As your maximum aerobic function develops—with months and years of training—your rate of progress will become more moderate.

Don't expect to see any radical improvements in your test times during the anaerobic and/or competitive segment of your yearly training plan. During those periods, you have amassed your maximum aerobic benefits. Yet, should your test course times become significantly slower in this phase, it's a good bet you are either overtrained (doing too many anaerobic workouts) or racing too frequently.

Recovery Time

The MAF test offers both novice and elite athletes the opportunity to evaluate another component in the fitness equation: recovery time, i.e., how long it takes the heart rate to return to normal after the stress of exercise. An effective training program should promote faster recovery time, regardless of the duration of your daily workout—it could be as short as 30 minutes or as long as 1½ hours.

Most cyclists are interested in getting in their miles. Yet, sometimes, that one workout, whether 5 miles or 50, could leave you overtrained if your body has not adequately recovered from previous exertions. This athletic malady, *over-training*, can easily be avoided by using the HRM in conjunction with the following guidelines:

☐ Make sure that you are aware of your initial heart rate before every workout.

☐ At the conclusion of each training session, adhere to the cool-down procedure as explained in Chapter 7. This ensures that your body will sufficiently recover from the effort of training.

☐ Observe your heart rate during the cool-down period. More than likely, the number of bpm will not have returned to the pre-exercise level. This is to be expected and indicates that you require more time to achieve full recovery.

Depending on your physical condition, it may take between 1 and 2 hours for your heart rate to get back to normal. And if you are new to the sport, your recovery may require an even longer term. If you are extremely fit, on the other hand, your pulse may drop down to its pre-exercise level within minutes. Bear in mind that the intensity of a ride does effect recovery time. An hour's hammering uphill, for instance, requires a longer recovery time than the same time spent on a slow, steady ride.

☐ Continue to wear the HRM for a couple of hours after your ride (this will require briefly removing the device while you're in the shower, unless you have a waterproof model). As you go through your post-exercise routine, you will probably find that your heart rate fluctuates slightly.

After a month or two of monitoring yourself in this fashion, you will have a good idea how long it takes you to recover from different types of exercise activities. With increasing fitness, your post-exercise pulse rate should move closer and closer to the pre-exercise level—as long as you don't suffer any physical problems.

Some athletes, however, may discover that their heart rate is not decreasing during the post-exercise period. There is nothing to worry about if that happens. Generally, it implies that the exercise was simply too stressful. Assuming this is the case, it will be reflected the next day by a higher than normal morning pulse rate, as discussed in the section *Morning Pulse*, below. If you find yourself in this situation, simply comply with the following prescription: Keep your heart rate at the lower end of the target zone on your next ride.

☐ When performing intervals and speed work, make sure that your heart rate drops down below your aerobic range after each hard effort. Let's say your target zone is 150–160 bpm, and the interval brings your heart rate up to 180 bpm. Don't engage in another interval until you see that your heart rate has settled back into the high 140s.

☐ Racers should follow the same basic recovery procedures as mentioned above. However, due to the physical demands of competition, their recovery times are usually longer. Often, the heart rates of cyclists who have participated in a race do not return to the pre-competition level for several hours—or even several days.

If you are a racer and your pulse remains above normal for more than a day or two, it may indicate one, or all, of the following problems: your racing form was inadequate (specifically, a greater aerobic base was required); the race was physically too demanding and, as a result, it may eventually cause illness or injury; or the recovery was incomplete for reasons that may include an injury, dehydration, or a nutritional deficiency.

☐ Wear your HRM for an entire day. When you are not exercising, turn the target zone signals off and regularly glance at the display. Using your morning pulse rate as the base figure, you can learn how much time it takes you to recover from the normal stress of things like walking to a neighborhood store, climbing a flight of stairs, etc.

Morning Pulse

More often than not, as you reach higher states of fitness, you will obtain correspondingly lower heart rate levels. This conditioning phenomenon can be easily observed by examining —and jotting down—your resting pulse throughout your yearly training program.

The best time to make this daily inquiry is after a long period of rest—specifically, right after waking up in the morning. What you will probably find is that your morning pulse becomes lower after several months of regular training.

If your exercise program is not yielding lower morning pulse figures, it may indicate that you have reached a plateau in your health and fitness. A plateau is a natural juncture in every athlete's training cycle. In time—somewhere between 2 and 4 months—your heart rate will begin to decline again.

Some people, however, will observe a steady rise in their morning heart rate. Should this happen, it is usually a sign that their health or fitness is deteriorating. If the morning pulse remains significantly higher than normal, it calls for the reduction in intensity of an athlete's training program. Should this revision fail to have a positive effect, then it may be necessary to seek out a sports physician's help.

It is not uncommon to wake up one day and find your morning pulse to be markedly higher than usual. Assume, for example, that your normal morning pulse is 52 bpm. Then, out of the blue, your regular 8 AM reading jumps to 72 bpm. When this happens—and even world-class athletes experience such moments—it's typically an indication that your body is being forced to work harder for some reason.

This unusual elevation in your normal morning pulse, then, provides an excellent opportunity to reflect on your current life situation. Maybe you are experiencing too much stress at home, on the job, or at school. Perhaps you are about to come down with a cold or the flu (two biochemical equivalents of a physical injury). Moreover, don't rule out the possibility that a soaring morning pulse could be a harbinger

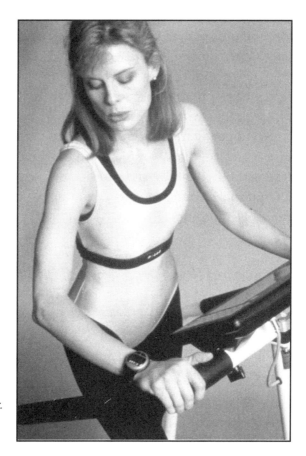

Fig. 8.7. Incoor training with the heart rate monitor. (photo courtesy Polar)

of a hidden stress—such as an impending injury from over-training.

Whenever your morning heart rate increases unexpectedly, it's wise to *stop, think, and respond quickly*. One appropriate response, as mentioned above, is to decrease the amount of time and the intensity of your scheduled workout. Another option—and only you can be the judge if this is necessary—is to eliminate that day's training session altogether. In all likelihood, either one of these conservative measures should bring your morning heart rate back to normal in a day or so.

Suppose, in an attempt to bring your morning pulse back to normal, you elect not to exercise for some time—be it as little as one day or as long as two weeks. When you do resume your training program, it's important to take it easy at first. Don't try to overcompensate for "lost" time or miles. Remember, your body and/or mind has just been through something. And a hasty effort to recover your form could precipitate the illness or injury you either had or just avoided.

By diligently monitoring and logging your morning pulse in a diary, you can become more sensitive to how you are feeling, both mentally and physically. Furthermore, this athletic journal will enable you to determine whether or not your fitness is improving.

Correlating Heart Rate, Speed, and Cadence

One of the most frequent questions asked by cyclists is what the ideal pedaling rate, or cadence, is. Traditionalists usually suggest a figure that ranges anywhere from 90 to 120 revolutions per minute. This suggestion, fails to consider an individual rider's heart rate. A more accurate way to determine optimum cadence starts by asking a different question: How fast can you ride most efficiently at your lowest heart rate?

You can obtain this very valuable information in one of two ways. First, by using an HRM that measures speed, cadence, and heart rate. A second option is to employ a basic HRM along with a cyclocomputer. By adhering to the following method, you can plot a graph that shows how fast you should be spinning the cranks.

☐ Ride over the test course at your maximum speed, at your maximum aerobic heart rate. (For the purpose of illustration, let's say you're able to travel 23 mph at 150 bpm, which puts you in the upper reaches of the target zone.)

☐ After the first test ride, give yourself adequate time to recover. How long this will take is determined by noting your active resting pulse—the number of heart bpm when walking, sitting, and standing—on the HRM. Try to relax during these moments. By concentrating on breathing rhythmically, you may be able to reduce your heart rate more rapidly. Indeed, this recovery technique can prove invaluable to racers.

☐ As soon as you have recovered, ride the test circuit at your maximum heart rate again. But this time upshift one gear as you try to increase your speed.

☐ If you are able to go faster, repeat steps 2 and 3 until your speed levels off or begins dropping. If your rides and recovery times total 30–45 minutes, you will probably register lower speeds as well as higher heart rates. Should this occur, it will invalidate the accuracy of your test results. So, if your cadence research lasts 30–45 minutes, stop and then resume it the next day.

☐ The test is over when you can no longer ride any faster. At this point, you have determined the most efficient cadence and gearing that will provide maximum speed while remaining in the target zone.

Once you have established these base figures, you might want to engage in further experimentation. Try adopting different hand positions on the handlebars (on the top, the brake levers and the drops), as well as saddle locations by sitting fore and aft. As you make each of these changes, pay close attention to your heart rate, speed, and cadence. This kind of fine-tuning will help optimize your cycling efficiency.

Aerobic Cycling Throughout the Yearly Training Program

Whether you are a novice or a veteran cyclist, the key to building and maintaining your aerobic base is to increase the amount of workout time. How much time you can spend exercising depends on your own particular circumstances: Each individual has a unique response to the physical stress of training, while personal commitments (work, family, school, etc.) also have to be taken into consideration. Given these fundamental provisos, some general rules will apply to most athletes:

☐ Regardless of how long you are able to exercise—whether 15 minutes or 5 hours—maintain that time frame for at least 2 weeks. This axiom should be adhered to before making any change in your training schedule. Staying with your current regimen for 14 days, before adding more time, gives your body an opportunity to adapt to new physical demands.

☐ In a training program that does not exceed 45 minutes, do not increase your training time—at any point—by more than 50 percent. If your training sessions are longer—say 1 hour—you can add 15-minute increments at 2-week intervals. This incremental approach will enable your body to benefit from the increased workload.

☐ Clinical experience with novice, recreational, and world-class cyclists and triathletes demonstrates that each group feels most comfortable—physiologically and psychologically—when they reach one of three primary riding time levels within each category: 45, 60, and 90 minutes for the novice rider; 60 minutes, 90 minutes, and 2 hours for the seasoned fitness cyclist or racer; and 3, 4, and 5 hours for the elite athlete.

When you progress to any one of these essential levels, you should remain there for at least 4 weeks before adding more time to your training sessions.

You may be quite content to exercise no longer than 45 minutes—and that is quite acceptable. You will still be rewarded with health and fitness benefits—providing you exercise in the target zone 5 times per week.

☐ Should you experience any physical problem during this training program, *stop immediately*. It's time to begin re-evaluating your exercise schedule. Frequently, aches and pains are a sign that you are doing too much too soon.

As both the beginner and the veteran spend more time on the bicycle, they can, for example, experience knee pain during and after riding. If this happens, take a few days off. And when you do get back in the saddle, ride for a month only at the level you had reached before you began to feel the discomfort. (This means that if you incurred knee pain upon moving your daily ride up from

1 hour to 1¼ hours, your rides for the next month should not exceed 1 hour.)

Should your pain either persist after spending several days not training, or return after you resume your scaled-down program, it's advisable to consult a sports physician. Being injured does not mean you should stop exercising. Rather, it means you have a physical problem that must be diagnosed and corrected promptly.

Chapter 9

Sample Training Programs

To get you started on the road to fitness and health, here are three introductory sample training programs, each geared to novice, intermediate, and advanced athletes. While these programs should be seen as practical examples that apply most specifically to cyclists, the same basic formats may be used by runners and swimmers, too. Table 9.1 on page 82 summarizes the typical programs for the aerobic phase of training.

Each of these introductory training programs is designed to build up your aerobic base. Once you have accomplished this without experiencing any physical problems, you're ready to move on to the next stage. During this 2-week period, you will be working on improving your aerobic speed.

Upon entering the aerobic speed phase, you are bridging the gap between casual exercise and outright training. Specifically, you will be spending more time riding.

☐ Once or twice a week, ride 2 times on the same day. During these AM and PM rides, stay in the lower range of your target zone.

☐ Once a week, ride 20%–25% longer than any of your other workouts, making sure that your heart rate remains in the middle to upper ranges of the target zone.

With these two alterations in mind, your training schedule —depending on your level of ability—may look like the ones outlined in Table 9.2 on page 83.

The day before your single longest ride should be spent off the bike, since it is essential to be well-rested to realize the maximum benefits from this longer workout. You should ride on the day after this effort—but be mindful to maintain a relatively slow cadence. Remaining active will help your body eliminate toxins.

Table 9.1 Aerobic training phase

Novice:

Mon	Tues	Wed	Thurs	Fri	Sat	Sun
off*	30 min	20 min	30 min	off*	30 min	20 min

* For the beginner working a typical full-time job, Monday and Friday are good 'off' days

Intermediate:

Mon	Tues	Wed	Thurs	Fri	Sat	Sun
60 min	90 min	60 min	90 min	60 min	off	120–150 min

Advanced:

Mon	Tues	Wed	Thurs	Fri	Sat	Sun
90 min	90 min	2 hrs	2 hrs	off	60 min	120–150 min

Note to Table 9.1. Whatever your level of proficiency, starting your aerobic phase of training should almost feel too easy. These schedules, like the ones that follow, can be modified by adjusting the days and times to fit your specific needs. However, try to maintain the same order.

Aerobic Intervals

Although most people assume interval training always involves anaerobic efforts, that is not the case. It is quite possible to perform intervals and still remain within aerobic parameters. Aerobic intervals can be done in the latter part of your first or second Aerobic Base periods. And because these workouts allow for a smooth transition to anaerobic training, they are particularly useful in a competitive training program.

Table 9.2 Speed phase

Novice:

Mon	Tues	Wed	Thurs	Fri	Sat	Sun
off	45 min	45 min (am) 45 min (pm)	75 min	off	75 min	30 min

Intermediate:

Mon	Tues	Wed	Thurs	Fri	Sat	Sun
60 min	90 min	60 min (am) 60 min (pm)	90 min	2 hrs	off	3 hrs

Advanced:

Mon	Tues	Wed	Thurs	Fri	Sat	Sun
60–90 min	90 min	2 hrs	3 hrs	2 hrs	off	3–5 hrs

Note to Table 9.2. As you progress in your aerobic phase, unless you're able to ride longer almost every day, it's a good idea to get a double workout once during the week. Even if one workout is indoors on a trainer, it can help stimulate the aerobic system and help you build a better base.

During the early phase of the Aerobic Base period, you may find it easy to achieve your MAF. Later on, as you ride faster upon approaching that level, you may experience a great degree of physical discomfort. More than likely, you'll perceive it as too hard to maintain that pace every day. As a result, you tend to work out at high speeds—but at lower heart rates. When this happens, you're ready to begin aerobic intervals.

An aerobic interval can be as short as 3 to 5 minutes or as long 10 to 15 minutes. Whichever time span you select, be realistic: Make sure you can sustain a pace that will keep you at your maximum aerobic heart rate. Even though this type of interval can bring you well above your normal speed, the workout will still be aerobic.

Sample 90-Minute Aerobic Interval Workout

For the sample interval, let's suppose that you can only ride at your maximum aerobic level of 145 bpm for 3 to 5 minutes. This, then, is the length of your interval. (When performing intervals, stay within your prescribed time, rather than establishing a numerical objective, such as 5 sets.) After each interval—which can be performed on a course that is either hilly or flat—slow your pace down to a comfortable heart rate (125–135 bpm in this example) for 6 to 10 minutes.

☐ 15 minute warmup period.

☐ 3–5 minutes at your maximum aerobic heart rate (MAF), i.e., 145 bpm in this example.

☐ 6–10 minutes at a more comfortable pace, 10–20 bpm lower than your maximum heart rate, i.e., 125–135 bpm in this example.

☐ Continue alternating between the pace at which you reach your maximum aerobic heart rate (145 bpm) and the one at which the heart rate is 10–20 bpm lower (125–135 bpm) until the start of the cool-down period.

☐ Finish off with a 15-minute cool-down period.

Anaerobic Training and Racing (April 1 to July 1)

During this period, you should do anywhere from 1 to 3 workouts per week that are designed to raise your heart rate above its Aerobic Maximum. Make no mistake, anaerobic training is extremely demanding. Yet all competitive cyclists should include these workouts in their schedule. Riders who fail to reach this equilibrium may incur poor health, lower levels of fitness, or a combination of these undesirable conditions.

Before scheduling your anaerobic sessions, consider the following guidelines:

☐ Typically, there should be at least 2, but no more than 3 anaerobic workouts per week.

☐ The day before an anaerobic effort should either be an *off* day on your training schedule, or it should be used for easy aerobic riding.

☐ Don't forget to warm up and cool down thoroughly on the days you perform your anaerobic routines.

☐ Anaerobic workouts should never be done on consecutive days.

Table 9.3 Anaerobic training phase

Novice:

Mon	Tues	Wed	Thurs	Fri	Sat	Sun
off or easy spin	Anaerobic: 15 min warmup 30-45 min anaerobic 15 min. cool-down	45 min	30 min	off	Anaerobic: 15 min warmup 45-60 min anaerobic 15 min cool-down	45 min

Intermediate:

Mon	Tues	Wed	Thurs	Fri	Sat	Sun
60 min	Anaerobic: 15 min warmup 60 min anaerobic 15 min cool-down	60 min	120 min	90 min	60n min	Anaerobic: 30 min warmup 2 hrs anaer. or race 30 min cool-down

Advanced:

Mon	Tues	Wed	Thurs	Fri	Sat	Sun
60-90 min	Anaerobic: 30 min warmup 2 hrs anaerobic 15 min on/off 30 min cool-down	60-90 min	Anaerobic same as Tues	60-90 min	60-90: min	3-5 hrs or race

Note to Table 9-3. Once you progress to the anaerobic phase, drop in those harder workouts on the most stress-free days. For most people, twice weekly is enough. If you compete, one of those anaerobic workouts can be an actual race. For the most advanced, three anaerobic days is the maximum. Never have two anaerobic days consecutively.

☐ The day following this intense effort, take only a short ride at an easy aerobic pace.

☐ A race is considered an anaerobic workout.

☐ The anaerobic period is at minimum 5 weeks in duration, assuming you don't experience any physical problems. It should not go beyond a maximum of 12–15 weeks.

☐ You are clearly anaerobic when your heart rate is above its Aerobic Maximum level. And, generally, whether you are mildly anaerobic or have reached your highest anaerobic state, many of the benefits are similar. Therefore, when you are doing anaerobic workouts, your pulse should not exceed your average competitive heart rate by more than 5 to 8 percent. (Competitive heart rate is highly individual, since it's an undefined number of bpm above a racer's target zone.) If you drive your pulse beyond this figure, you are not only wasting energy, but running the risk of overtraining as well.

Sample anaerobic programs for each level of proficiency are listed in Table 9.3 on page 86.

Anaerobic Intervals

Anaerobic intervals can be executed either in the hills or on the flats, as long as you abide by the guideline listed under the last point above: Don't exceed your competitive heart rate by more than 5 to 8 percent. The only cyclists exempted from this caveat are those racers who are attempting to improve their sprinting techniques. Usually, sprinting in a race demands an all-out effort for no more than 500 meters. And, during this short burst, it's highly impractical not to permit your heart rate to rise above the 5 to 8 percent boundary. But even burly-thighed sprinters must be careful not to push themselves beyond a certain limit.

Let's say that 8 percent above your competitive heart rate lies between 175 and 180 bpm. After 4 sets of sprint intervals, your pulse has been consistently in this range. It's a good bet that you have already obtained the maximum fitness benefits from your workout—and to ride another set could harm your body.

As you continue with anaerobic training, the HRM will tell you whether or not you're making fitness advances. Assume, for instance, that your maximum heart rate rises to 180 bpm at the beginning of your interval practice. There are two ways of gauging your progress after a month or two of performing these workouts.

First, you can consistently demonstrate the ability to complete your interval sets at the same times—over the same distance—at lower heart rates. A second, and even better, indication of your improving fitness is this: You can perform your interval sets in faster times, over the same distance, at the same heart rate—in this case 180 bpm.

Sometimes, your heart rate may increase, or your times may get slower when doing interval workouts. When this happens, you should ask yourself the following questions:

☐ Have you made a mistake in your calculations and come up with too high a figure for your maximum heart rate?

☐ Are you performing too many intervals during a session?

☐ Have you gone beyond the recommended number of days for your interval program?

☐ Are you doing too much anaerobic training in general?

☐ Are you failing to consume enough fluids during these demanding efforts?

In all likelihood, if you responded *Yes* to any or all of these questions, you will have discovered the source(s) of your declining speed and/or rising heart rate. Some adjustment(s), therefore, will be necessary.

Weight Training

Weight training, according to most bicycle training manuals, should be performed during the off season. This is incorrect. Pumping iron, because it demands that your muscles produce both power and strength, is clearly an anaerobic exercise. This is true whether you are doing numerous light weight repetitions or fewer repetitions with heavier weights.

The HRM has two primary functions during weightlifting sessions. It will remind you to warm up and cool down thoroughly as well as ensure that your recovery time between sets is sufficient.

Throughout the weight workout itself, heart rate is not a valid means of distinguishing aerobic from anaerobic. That's because, in this instance, your pulse will reach a plateau very quickly. Yet, before this happens, the repetitions are over—or, more precisely, your muscles fatigue and you stop lifting. As a result, you don't obtain an accurate reading from the HRM due to the short time you are actually exercising.

The one exception to this assertion applies to the novice athlete who has just started a training program. In this case, if you lift weights, your heart rate will rise rapidly and may exceed its aerobic maximum before finishing the workout. Novices are better off concentrating on building their aerobic base, an objective that will not be achieved by lifting weights.

Aerobic Base Period (A Break from Anaerobic Training and Racing), July 1 to August 15

The value of the second Aerobic Base period for competitive cyclists is twofold. First, it helps them recoup some of their energies expended on races during the spring and early summer. Second, this break can enable racers to peak for the big events that frequently close out their racing calendar. For the fitness enthusiast, this period is a welcome respite from the strain of performing intense, anaerobic interval workouts.

If you ride to stay in shape, you will probably experience no difficulty in making this transition. Racers, however, may find that this second Aerobic Base period does pose some logistical problems. Often, due to the complexity and fullness of their competitive program, it will be hard to set aside the time to adequately recharge their aerobic system. To avoid missing out on this important training phase, racers should take time at the beginning of the season to factor this period into the yearly calendar.

Resumption of Anaerobic Training and Racing, August 1 to November 15

Throughout this 3½-month period, both the competitive and the fitness cyclist should repeat the sequence of exercises outlined in the first anaerobic segment. This is an opportune moment to make any needed adjustments in your training plan.

This is where your training diary will come in very handy. If you have been faithfully recording and entering your morning pulse, along with your workout and/or competition data, you can easily determine whether you are progressing, regressing, or plateauing. But before modifying your workout schedule, make the following investigation:

☐ Is your morning heart rate consistently higher, lower, or stable?

☐ Throughout your day, do you feel that you have more or less energy?

☐ Have you been free of injury and illness? Or have you been caught in a web of colds and the flu, and/or experiencing some serious aches and pains?

☐ Are the times on your test course during MAF-test rides higher, lower, or remaining constant?

☐ How are you performing during Aerobic Interval workouts —faster, slower, or unchanged?

☐ When doing Anaerobic Intervals, is your heart rate higher, lower, or stable? Is your speed holding steady, or are you riding faster or slower?

☐ If you have been racing, it's important to consider your level of experience. Usually, novice racers can't expect to make the same gains as their more experienced counter-parts. Bearing this in mind, do you see any changes in your performance? Are you getting more or fewer top-10 fin-ishes? Are you coming in with the bunch, or ending up in "no man's land"? Are you able to cover the crucial breaks, or are you getting dropped? Do you have the strength to initiate attacks? When the race enters the hills, can you stay up front with leaders, or do you become a caboose?

Upon carefully appraising your responses, you will know whether or not to use this second anaerobic period to maintain or modify your training regimen.

The ideal training program should promote your health as well as your conditioning. This means you should not engage in any activities that could compromise your well-being in exchange for potential fitness benefits. In fact, if you follow a course that keeps this principle in mind, you can establish complete body harmony.

Chapter 10

The HRM in Competition

A heart rate monitor is extremely beneficial for athletes who engage in competition. By periodically noting their heart rates during a race, they can conserve precious energy as well as maximize performance.

Whatever kind of race you compete in, it's only natural that your heart rate will be constantly varying upward and downward. An all-out sprint, for example, obviously will send your pulse rocketing skyward, while sitting in the pack for an extended period of time could find your heart rate numbers plummeting below the target zone. This kind of ebbing and flowing of your heart rate is very costly from an energy conservation standpoint. Most significantly, it saps your stamina and, ultimately, causes fatigue to come on quicker.

Figure 8.5, in Chapter 8, shows the heart rate of a competitor throughout a race. Ideally, you want to maintain a pace that allows you to maintain a steady heart rate throughout the event. Sometimes, this may seem impossible—as when climbing a very steep hill, for example. Yet, if you moderate your efforts on a demanding climb, you can expect to gain some advantages over your opponents later in the race. Your heart rate will remain within the target zone and, consequently, you will have more strength left when approaching the finish line.

Usually, racers who are not strong climbers are reluctant to adopt a less than all-out strategy on the ascent. They feel that holding back will cause them to lose contact with either the peloton or the lead group. If you don't have the kind of legs that allow you to dance up mountains, you will do well to adopt traditional bike racing tactics.

Before the race, scout the course and learn where the major climbs are located. Then, during the event, as you approach each ascent, move to the front of the group you are riding with. As you begin climbing, make sure you sustain a rhythm that keeps you within the target zone. Frequently, this very basic maneuver may serve to either cut your losses or keep you up with the race leaders. What is almost certain, however, is that you will have conserved a lot of energy—which can be utilized after you crest the summit.

Commonly, those racers who go beyond their target zone's upper limit during an all-out ascent have to coast down, freewheeling to recover on the descent. But by riding within the competitive target zone, you will have another option: You can shift into a higher gear and begin charging down the hill.

The Individual and Team Time Trial

A heart rate monitor is a boon to riders who plan to enter either an individual or a team time trial. During training rides, you can use it in conjunction with a stopwatch to improve your form and evaluate your equipment. Wearing an HRM on practice runs will help determine the best saddle position to keep you in the target zone. Furthermore, you can use the device to evaluate which handlebars, crank lengths, wheels, helmet, clothing, and even which bike will save you precious second—which will pay off on the day of the race.

When it comes to the target zone during a competitive time trial, you do not have to be all that concerned about the upper limit of your heart rate. That is because you should primarily be concerned with squeezing out every drop of energy from the human engine. In time trials, you should be neither surprised nor worried if you are able to push your heart rate above its normal maximum.

Yet in order to get the most out of your body during this "race of truth," pay close attention to the HRM when warming up. Take at least 15 minutes to raise your heart rate to its highest aerobic level. Then maintain a pace that pegs the pulse at this figure for another 10 to 15 minutes. Follow this up with several short sprints and recoveries that allow your heart rate to drop just below the target zone. The virtue of this warmup routine will be evident soon after the event begins: In just a few minutes, you should be able to comfortably pedal at your racing cadence.

The Stage Race

During a stage race, cyclists are going through a unique situation. For several consecutive days—or weeks—they find themselves continuously preparing for competition, expending energy, and recovering. Using an HRM as a biofeedback unit can help you achieve your best results throughout these physically and mentally demanding contests.

Regardless of a stage race's duration, an intelligent rider must formulate a strategy. This strategy, however, goes beyond fundamental cycling tactics. In order to be successful— as well as survive the ordeal—you have to pay careful attention to your body. Observing your heart rate from morning to night can help you decide whether this is a day to hold back or to attack.

When competing in a multi-day event, it is crucial to check your morning pulse on a daily basis. Just as in training, this figure is an accurate barometer of your physical condition. Be aware of the fact that, as you spend day after day at or above your maximum aerobic pace (MAP), there will be a corresponding rise in your morning heart rate. Still, if you happen to notice a sharp rise in your heart rate upon waking up, try to play it conservatively during the day's event. On the other hand, if you are in really good form, your morning pulse may be the same as usual. When you record such readings, you can approach the day's stage with the well-founded confidence that your body possesses a sufficient reserve of energy.

At the onset of the race, keep your eye on your HRM. Invariably, after many miles of pedaling, you will see a rise in your pulse. If you notice that you're riding more slowly and inefficiently while in the target zone, it's a sign that your body is not feeling strong. Therefore this is not the time for aggressive cycling. Instead, sit in for as long as possible, conserving your energy for the race's key breakaway. But suppose you can comfortably maintain your pace with heart rate numbers that lie in the lower portion of the target zone. This is a good indication that your body has ample energy and, should the opportunity present itself, you could go on the offensive.

After the day's stage is completed, don't forget to monitor your daytime resting pulse. This will provide you with valuable information about your recovery process. By observing your heart rate after hard training rides and single-day races, you should be thoroughly aware of how your body responds to the stress placed upon it. If you are obtaining your usual numbers upon finishing a stage, there's no need to alter the strategy you have planned for the next day. However, should you see that the resting pulse is higher than normal, it's advisable to moderate your effort.

By monitoring your heart rate before, during, and after every stage, you can enhance your performance and minimize the chance of injury or illness.

Irrespective of the competitive event, many racers make an all too common mistake: They ride too fast relative to their ability. Although this is understandable, given the psychological investment most riders have made in winning, you can reach more of your potential by not going all out at the sound of the starter's pistol. Be aware of your heart rate for the first few miles, making sure you remain in the lower portion of the target zone. This conservative approach will enable you to ride within yourself. Unfortunately, while many racers understand this principle, they have quite a lot of difficulty putting it into practice.

Competition Recommendations

The purpose of these recommendations is to allow your body and mind to function optimally. And on the day of a big race, who doesn't want that to happen? The means to achieving this highly desirable end is to eliminate much of the structural, chemical, and mental stress a racer experiences before, during, and after competition.

The Week Before the Race

Suppose you've been very disciplined. For the past several months you have scrupulously adhered to your training regimen. Consequently, with a contest only 7 days away, you know that you have the mental and physical capabilities that could result in a top-10 placing—or a possible victory. But even if you are in peak condition, you can still turn in a terrible performance by failing to follow any one of several pre-race guidelines.

Generally, the body doesn't like to go through severe changes. So don't change any of the positive habits you have formed throughout the yearly training plan during the week leading up to your event. Yet in order to fine-tune your conditioning, specific modifications will be necessary:

☐ In the week preceding the competition, slightly decrease your regular cycling mileage. Make sure, too, that all your rides are relatively easy ones. The exception to this, however, is when your fitness schedule calls for riding anaerobically. In this instance, limit yourself to one hard effort 4 days before the race.

☐ Being in great physical shape alone doesn't guarantee a good competitive performance. The mind also comes into play. Remember, you do have control over your thoughts. Try to ignore subconscious negative thoughts. ("I'm afraid he/she is much better than I am," "I really can't do this," etc.) As each day brings the race closer, become more mentally focused on the impending effort. Be optimistic but realistic. Maintaining a balanced psychological state can affect your race results.

The Day Before the Race: To Ride or Not to Ride?

Many cyclists perform better when they don't ride on the day before a race. Depending on how your body feels, as well as your level of confidence, two days off might also be appropriate. Don't be afraid to experiment with these suggestions—however, putting in the miles at the "twelfth hour" is really of no benefit. Still, if you're tense before the event, you might take your bike out for an easy spin. Be aware of the fact that even professional riders experience some anxiety prior to an important race. It's all right to be a little edgy before your event—and knowing how to manage this emotion can be an invaluable asset.

Chapter 11

The HRM in Running and Swimming

As mentioned previously, cyclists of all levels can derive health as well as fitness benefits from running and swimming. And since both of these activities are fundamentally aerobic, swimmers and runners will definitely profit by training with an HRM.

Athletes who plan on focusing all of their energies on either running or swimming should adopt the same Yearly Training Plan as cyclists. Like cyclists, they must attain a balance between health and fitness by incorporating aerobic base periods with anaerobic workouts and/or competition.

Fig. 11.1. Running with the Sensor Dynamics ProSport. This waterproof 7-function HRM incorporates a split-screen setting that displays the current heart rate in addition to the selected function. (photo courtesy Sensor Dynamics)

Running

As you become a more proficient runner, the time and intensity of your workout will become greater. Running with an HRM, in the target zone, ensures that as the training demands increase, the stress on your body will remain constant.

Here's how this works: Let's say, for the purpose of illustration, that you are able to run 3 miles in 27 minutes, keeping your heart rate in a target zone of 130 bpm. Two months later, it's quite possible that you will be able to run the same distance—at the same heart rate—in about 25 minutes and 30 seconds.

Runners, like cyclists, can measure their aerobic progression through the self-administration of the MAF test. When it comes to conducting the MAF test, a runner has it somewhat easier than a bike rider. That's because an important variable—the bicycle—has been eliminated. Moreover, this makes the test for running a bit more accurate, since the freewheeling, or coasting, factor is not applicable to the activity. However, other previously mentioned issues, such as climate, mental and physical states, etc., must still be taken into consideration.

The best location for a runner to perform the MAF test is a quarter-mile (or 400 meter) track. This facility will be easier to

---

Table 11.1 Sample MAF test pattern

Mile	Time
1	9:00
2	9:12
3	9:18
4	9:25
5	9:38

find than a velodrome, since your local high school or college probably has one. If locating a track does prove impossible, measure out a "user-friendly" loop or stretch of road that is one mile long.

Upon arriving at your test course, begin by warming up for 10 to 15 minutes. At the end of this time, your heart rate should reach the lower threshold of the target zone. You are now ready to begin running at your maximum aerobic level.

With your HRM in the stopwatch mode, see how much time it takes to cover a mile at your maximum aerobic level. If you are able to maintain this pace for 5 miles—and don't go beyond this distance—clock each mile separately, and mentally record the figures. Should you be unable to sustain your aerobic maximum for 5 miles, then only run 2 miles, making sure to note your split times. Perform the MAF test once every 3 weeks. This will provide concrete information as to whether you are progressing, plateauing, or regressing.

As you perform the MAF test, you will probably see the time for each subsequent mile gradually increase. This is normal, due to accumulated fatigue. If you run the first mile in 9 minutes, for example, the second mile may take 9 minutes and 12 seconds to cover. A typical MAF-test pattern looks like the one illustrated in Table 11.1.

Table 11.2 Sample training diary entries

Month	Heart Rate bpm	MAF (mile pace)
1	135	9:48
2	135	9:21
3	135	9:01
4	135	8:55
5	135	8:40

Generally, in a 5-mile MAF test, the difference in time between mile 1 and mile 5 should not be more than 45 to 60 seconds. If the differences in your test results exceed this time span, it usually means that running this distance is creating more stress than your body can handle. The best response to this situation is to restrict your MAF test to 2 miles.

Some runners who take the 5-mile test may find that their times for the first 2 miles are exactly the same, or they are able to run the second mile at a higher speed than the first one. The implication of either of these results is that the runner needs a longer warmup period. (The same inference can be made when such times are recorded during the 2-mile MAF test.)

As you continue with your running program, you should begin to see gradual improvements in your maximum aerobic efficiency. By employing an HRM, you can objectively determine whether or not you are progressing. The training diary entries of a runner who is making gains commonly looks something like those summarized in Table 11.2. The two significant features in this log are the progressively faster times for the run and the stable heart rate.

As the months pass and your maximum aerobic efficiency improves, you will reach a point where your test times level off. There's no need for any concern. You have simply reached a natural plateau. What this means is that you have obtained the maximum aerobic benefits of the base period, and it's appropriate to begin your anaerobic workouts.

It's not uncommon to reach your aerobic peak several weeks before you are scheduled to begin anaerobic training. When this happens, it's wise to disregard the calendar—or else your body could become anaerobically deficient.

Anaerobic Workouts

Whether you are training for short or long distance races, eventually you should get on the track and perform interval workouts. During these strong efforts, the HRM's primary function is to ensure that your recovery is adequate. A quick glance at the monitor after each interval dash will inform you when you're ready to go again.

Using an HRM in this manner flies in the face of the traditional approach to doing intervals. Customarily, runners

---

Case History: Peter's Plateau

Peter was an extremely fit runner, who after following a training program he had read of in a running magazine, seemed to reach a plateau in performance. His 5 km times were stuck at around 16 minutes and he began to require 10 hours of sleep each night—but was still tired all day. Furthermore, he was coming down with a cold every 3 months, almost like clockwork.

All of these circumstances led Peter to consult a sports medicine doctor. He explained that his pace was close to 6 minutes per mile on easy training days, and nearly 1 minute faster during harder workouts. When the physician asked Peter to perform the MAF test for 3 miles, he recorded times of 7:41, 7:49, and 7:58.

Given these results, Peter was advised to use an HRM while working out in an effort to slow down his pace. Shortly after employing this device, his aerobic training time progressed to 6:05, which enabled him to run a 5 km race in 15:30—a personal best. Better yet, he no longer needed as much sleep, while his energy and health reached a new peak.

---

conform to the following routine: They pound the track at their race pace for a quarter of a mile and then jog for 220 yards. This format—which can continue for 30 to 45 minutes—is based on the assumption that each 220-yard jog brings runners back to their recovery point. While this may work for some athletes, others find this recovery procedure unsatisfactory.

By employing an HRM, you can practice two other interval methods that will make your recovery period—as well as the rest of this workout—more effective:

☐ After warming up, perform a quarter-mile interval at your anaerobic speed. Anaerobic speed is slightly faster than your racing pace and should not exceed your maximum aerobic heart rate by more than 15 percent (if you are training correctly, these two factors should coincide). Upon completing the interval, slow down and begin jogging. As you jog, keep an eye on the HRM. You will be ready to run your next anaerobic interval when your pulse drops just below your aerobic range.

If your pulse doesn't fall, or remains in the target zone for more than a minute, it means you did the anaerobic interval much too rapidly: Slow down.

As you proceed with the anaerobic workout, you will probably find that the time it takes to jog and recover will become progressively longer. This is a normal response to the intensity of anaerobic activity. When you find that your recovery requires the same time and/or distance as the interval itself, you have achieved the maximum benefits from the workout. At this point, begin cooling down.

☐ The second anaerobic interval method is based solely on time and heart rate. Because of this, you can do these workouts either on the road or on the track. After warming up, perform an interval for a specific period of time—say one minute. Then jog for as long as it takes to bring your heart rate just below its maximum aerobic range. When this occurs, repeat the interval. Continue this procedure for no more than 45 minutes, or until the interval and recovery times are almost the same. Some runners will adapt better to this format, since they are neither distracted by the necessity of counting laps nor bound by the imposition of a specified distance.

As you proceed through the anaerobic period, you will find that your maximum aerobic efficiency remains at a peak level.

Table 11.3 Race Pace Predicted

MAP per mile	5 km Race per mile	time
10:00	7:30	23:18
9:00	7:00	21:45
8:30	6:45	20:58
8:00	6:30	20:12
7:30	6:00	18:38
7:00	5:30	17:05
6:30	5:15	16:19
6:00	5:00	15:32
5:45	4:45	14:45
5:30	4:30	13:59
5:00	4:20	13:28
5:00	4:15	13:12

And, upon resuming aerobic base training again, you will be able to achieve even faster MAF-test times.

Maximum Aerobic Efficiency and its Relationship to Competition

There is a clear relationship between maximum aerobic efficiency and your ability to perform at a specific competitive pace for specified distances. A case study of a runner's maximum aerobic pace (MAP) and race pace is indicated in Table 11.3.

The significance of this example is that it demonstrates that the runner has achieved an excellent balance between health and fitness during his competitive period. If you are not obtaining similar results, it may be an indication that your body is either structurally or chemically imbalanced. Again, remedial action is called for. Start by re-evaluating your training program and life-style. If this fails to correct the problem, it's advisable to seek out medical assistance.

But suppose you are able to complete your MAF-test run in 8 minutes—and can race a 5 km course in close to 18 minutes (a time that is better than a 5:30 pace per mile). While you might be pleased with this competitive outing, it really isn't all that positive. It demonstrates that, considering your aerobic ability, you are still capable of running faster. When your MAF is 8 minutes per mile, you should not be able to race a 5 km event in a time that eclipses 20 minutes, or at about a 6:30 pace.

To have the capacity to run faster than your body would normally permit signals that you are a candidate for injury or illness. If your anaerobic capacity is greater than your aerobic capacity, it means you have a chemical imbalance. This kind of dissonance often leads to a physical imbalance that can then traumatize the body.

Swimming

For swimmers—especially those who don't have access to a coach—the HRM is indispensable, because it will encourage them to train harder and more efficiently. Of course, you must make sure you select an HRM that is guaranteed to be waterproof.

Swimming tends to limit gravity's stress on the athlete; the only resistance a swimmer faces is the water itself. Because of this phenomenon, swimmers have to expend a lot of effort to get their heart rate into the target zone. Also, to produce an exceptional performance in the water, a swimmer, like a cyclist, must exhibit a high level of technical proficiency.

MAF Test for Swimmers

Just as with cycling and running, you can employ the MAF test to monitor your swimming improvements. An indoor

Fig. 11.2. The HRM is useful in swimming too. (photo courtesy Sensor Dynamics)

pool at your local Y, club, high school, or college is an excellent place to conduct this test. Usually, the environment factors—lane distance and temperature—remain constant.

Swimmers have a choice of administering the MAF test in one of two ways. They can either time themselves over a specified distance—say 1,000 yards—or for the number of laps they plan on swimming. Regardless of which procedure is used, it's essential to try to keep the heart rate within the target zone.

It's very simple for swimmers to determine whether or not they are making training progress: After several months of conducting the MAF test, you should be able to swim the same number of laps—or distance—in faster times at the same heart rate.

Suppose it takes you 12 minutes and 30 seconds to swim twenty 50-yard laps at your maximum aerobic heart rate of 145 bpm when you first start conducting the MAF test. After a month of adhering to your training regimen, you might be able to cover this same distance—at the same maximum aerobic heart rate—in, say, 12 minutes flat. A month later, it would not be inconceivable for your heart rate to remain at 145 bpm, while your time for these twenty 50-yard laps dropped to 11 minutes and 45 seconds.

By contrast, if your times for this distance become slower, it may be indicative of any one of the following problems: an impending injury or illness, overtraining, or too much stress in your living circumstances. Upon ascertaining the cause(s) of your regression, it's essential to make the appropriate revisions. This could mean a modification of your diet, life-style, or training program.

Anaerobic Intervals and Competition

Novice swimmers who have completed their base training may easily surpass aerobic maximum heart rates when doing anaerobic intervals or engaging in competition. If this is your situation, the HRM will only be beneficial for warming up, cooling down and recovery periods during interval sessions.

Generally, using an HRM during a race is impractical. Looking at the unit while churning through the water would more than likely disrupt the mechanics of swimming. Yet the HRM can be very helpful if you participate in triathlons or several events on the same day. In these cases, the device will help you relax as well as evaluate your heart rate while preparing yourself for the next competitive segment.

Triathlons and Biathlons

Those athletes who become proficient in cycling, running, and swimming can experience the challenge and excitement of multi-sport competition. Usually, a biathlon event follows the sequence of run-bike-run; while a triathlon begins with a swim, then has a bike leg, and concludes with a run. A heart rate monitor can help you do your best in all of these events.

As with other forms of endurance contests, use the monitor to help you warm up thoroughly. Once the contest gets under way, the device can remind you to maintain your maximum racing heart rate. As mentioned previously, this is a more efficient way of competing than having your pulse go through peaks and valleys—which, ultimately, is a waste of energy.

Let's assume, for example, your maximum racing heart rate is 165 bpm. During competition, you don't want to deviate more than 5 bpm above or below that figure. Yet, not only do you feel very good early in the race, but your heart rate is 5 bpm lower than normal. If you are fortunate enough to be in this position, it should provide an incentive to push yourself harder.

Conversely, just after a race begins, you may find yourself in a radically different situation. Along with feeling bad, you may discover that your heart rate is well above the normal target zone. When this happens, it's crucial to slow down. Failure to do so could result in not finishing your event or turning in a sub-par performance.

In order to do well in a triathlon and biathlon, you must make smooth transitions. As you gain experience in these events, you will learn that the key to doing this is to stay relaxed. While you rapidly shift from one discipline to another, look at your HRM: It will remind you to breathe deeply and stay calm, which will both conserve energy and bring your heart rate down.

Chapter 12

The HRM in Other Sports

In virtually any sport or physical activity, the heart rate monitor can be an invaluable asset. For those participating in aerobics, roller blading, cross-country skiing, and snow shoeing, a monitor can regulate your warmup and cool-down phases as well as keep you either aerobic or anaerobic in accordance with your training program.

In other words, athletes engaged in these activities should adhere to the exercise principles outlined in this book's previous chapters. And that includes the administration of the MAF

Fig. 12.1. Indoor fitness training with the HRM. (photo courtesy Sensor Dynamics)

test, too, as a way to both establish your fitness benchmark and to determine your progress.

Devotees of golf and any of the racket sports—tennis, racketball, squash, paddle tennis—or even bowling, can improve their performances by utilizing a heart rate monitor. It can enable the participants in these endeavors to prepare their bodies—and their minds—for the challenges competition offers.

To establish a firm physical groundwork for any of these games, you'll need to choose another form of exercise in order to build up your aerobic system. Some individuals prefer walking. Others jog, run, ride a bike, or go in for swimming or aerobics.

As for using the heart rate to cultivate the mental side of your game, it is essential to read Chapter 14, *Breathing: The Forgotten Component*. By learning how to breathe correctly, you will be able to lower your heart rate—when it's appropriate. Cross-country skiing biathletes apply this technique to calm down before firing rounds from their rifles into targets.

Proper breathing, in conjunction with a heart rate monitor, can help you compose yourself prior to playing a big point in tennis or when standing over a crucial putt in golf. Usually, within 45 seconds of taking slow, deep breaths you'll see a marked decrease in your pulse. If you think this is poppycock, you can prove it to yourself. Just wear a monitor during a match, breathe correctly, and observe whether your heart rate falls or rises.

Below is a more specific training synopsis of these "other sports" and how the heart rate monitor can elevate your performance.

Aerobics

Frequently, any group-led activity provides advantages to its members, particularly from a psychological standpoint. Many exercisers enjoy working out with others of the same persuasion, and this social dimension contributes to maintaining a consistent training schedule. Yet exercising en masse can foster problems—such as those that might occur in an aerobic class, for example.

Even Jane Fonda would agree that not everyone who's dancing or doing step routines is capable of performing these activities at the same degree of exertion. Some of these lycra-clad people will actually be aerobic, but others on the same

Fig. 12.2. The HRM will serve you well when doing aerobic exercises. However, if you work out close to another participant wearing one too, the electronic signals may interfere with one another. (photo courtesy Polar)

floor will find themselves anaerobic. There are two avenues out of this unhealthy situation: Select a class that's suitable to your fitness level and/or use a heart rate monitor. The monitor will ensure the preservation of your individual effort during a group workout.

On the other hand, if everyone in an aerobics class exercises their right to wear a heart rate monitor, it may foment the problem of transmission interference; i.e., your receiver could display the pulse of the person moving next to you. (See Chapter 6, *Evaluating Heart Rate Monitors*).

Fortunately, there are a couple of ways to skirt this issue. Be a little bit territorial. Make sure no one else with a monitor comes within a good 6 to 8 feet of you. Also make sure to keep at least that distance—perhaps more—from fitness buffs on electrical exercise equipment (treadmills, stair climbers, ergometers). These are your only options until digital, radio-frequency monitors hit the market.

In-line Skating

In-line skating is one of the fastest-growing sports in America today. As with other athletic disciplines, a heart rate monitor can definitely upgrade the conditioning that results from this activity, in the context of a well thought out workout program. Stick to the same schedules this book suggests for runners and cyclists. And don't omit taking the MAF test.

Still, skaters travelling at breakneck speeds will have some difficulty observing their heart rates. It's often hard to see the wristwatch's visual display while your arms are rapidly swinging from side to side. To slow your arms in order to peek at the pulse will subtly throw off your gait. In addition, the low beeps of the monitor's auditory target zone alarms can be obliterated by the noise of the wheels rumbling along the tarmac. There are several possible remedies to this situation, though. For those wanting to "see" their pulse with their ears, buckle the receiver to your shirt collar or to your helmet. Another option is to attach the receiver to the roller blades' laces. Then, with a quick glance, you can easily be aware of your heart rate.

Cross-country skiing

You have probably seen proficient cross-country skiers gliding across the snow's surface. This graceful sliding action makes cross-country skiing, like walking, a low gravity-stress activity. As a result, most reasonably fit people with good technique experience lower heart rates. Yet, as with walking, this measurement is bound to rise when athletes schuss faster and farther.

But before rushing into this winter sport, it's important to build up a solid aerobic base. More than likely, this means being involved in an additional activity—although you could construct an aerobic foundation on just cross-country skiing. If you do choose to ski yourself into shape, though, just make sure to do it slowly.

Regardless of your fitness, it won't be easy to take the MAF test because snow conditions vary throughout the season, and even from day to day. But if the snow remains consistent, skiing on a flat stretch of terrain will enable you to perform the test—using the same principles as runners and cyclists. Furthermore, the rest of the running and cycling programs— aerobic and anaerobic phases, along with competition— applies to cross-country skiers.

The arm movements in cross-country skiing aren't optimal for heart rate tracking. On top of that, wearing gloves over the receiver muffles the target zone's warning beepers. So, like roller bladers, you'll want to move the wristwatch closer to your ears. If you have a waterproof model, you could attempt lacing the receiver to one of your ski boots, also.

Snow Shoeing

Snow shoeing is an extremely demanding sport. Except for descents, there's little or no sliding, and if you lack excellent technique, get ready for some rough going. Still, with only a fair amount of practice, you can master the art of "floating" on snow.

A snow shoer's exercise program—aerobic and anaerobic phases, the MAF test, along with competition—mirrors, for all intents and purposes, that of the cross-country skier. Snow shoers can also adopt the regimen of either the competitive or noncompetitive walker.

Racket Sports: tennis, racketball, paddle tennis and squash

Anybody playing a racket sport can boost the level of their game by using a heart rate monitor. For starters, employ it in the off-season to build your aerobic base by walking, running, swimming, cycling, or a combination of these activities. And while perfecting your strokes during this period, wear a monitor to warm up, cool down, and to insure that you stay within aerobic limits.

As you become more aerobically fit, you'll be able to perform with greater intensity without a significant rise in your pulse. This could make all the difference in the world in determining a match's outcome.

Once the competitive season is at hand, continue to wear the heart rate monitor. Use it for those hard, grueling workouts; use it for warming up with an opponent; and use it for cooling down after a contest.

What's more, during an event, the monitor can help regulate your stress and energy expenditure. By remaining aware of your pulse, you can attempt to dictate the pace of the match in response to the needs of your body. After a particularly long point, for example, let the heartrate drop below its aerobic level prior to resuming play.

This same strategy will come in handy when you're serving. A lower pulse indicates a high state of relaxation—which can only contribute to better accuracy in ball placement. Also, pay close attention to your monitor between games and sets. By breathing correctly, you can lower your heart rate and ward off fatigue, a factor that often determines a match's winner and loser.

Golf and Bowling

While both golf and bowling are games of technique, they rely much more on mental "conditioning" than on physical fitness. Players of both sports can still derive enormous benefits from utilizing a heart rate monitor to keep stress at bay and sustain an attitude of dynamic relaxation. Cultivating this focused but internally "loose" posture can add points to a bowler's score sheet and reduce a golfer's stroke total.

The first step to achieving this result during pressure-packed, competitive situations begins with training yourself to stay cool during practice rounds or frames. The routine you adopt during these dress rehearsals is the same one you'll follow in competitive situations.

So, after strapping on the heart rate monitor, take a walk for 15 to 30 minutes to elevate your pulse to about 20 bpm below the target zone. (See *Walking With the Heart Rate Monitor* in Chapter 13.) A warmup will improve circulation as well as stimulate the fat-burning aerobic system, which helps coordination—and, yes, promotes relaxation.

Prior to delivering or hitting the ball, concentrate on breathing properly. Notice your heart rate. In all likelihood, it will diminish and then level off. This figure is your "ideal" playing pulse, a zone you want to maintain every time you hit or toss the ball.

When sitting in between frames or strolling to the next shot, use the monitor along with the right breathing pattern to keep your mind quiet. Tension-inducing chatter produces a higher heart rate, which invariably detracts from your performance.

Simply put, the heart rate monitor is generating biofeedback that will help you play at your best, and it can be used in any sport that requires physical output for a prolonged period of time.

Chapter 13

The HRM in Walking and Physical Fitness

Walking is a valuable physical activity for the competitive and noncompetitive athlete alike. That's because a vigorous stroll—believe it or not—may burn a higher percentage of fat than most other exercises. This is due to the fact that walking is usually a low-intensity activity and, as a result, engages only

Fig. 13.1. Even in low-impact activities like walking and hiking, the HRM is a useful tool. Remember that even people of the same age can have widely different target zones. It all depends on your general health, fitness and athletic goals. (photo courtesy Polar)

119

the small aerobic muscle fibers. Frequently, it's these muscles that don't receive stimulation during workouts of higher intensity.

Walking is also one of the easiest and best ways to kick off a regular exercise regimen. It's inexpensive, since the only equipment you need to purchase are a pair of appropriate walking shoes. (Those people who want footwear with all the bells and whistles will pay accordingly, however.) It's simple, because—except for mastering the skill of breathing rhythmically—there's really not a lot of technique to master. And because this exercise puts relatively low stress on the body, a walker rarely suffers nagging injuries.

A person who takes up walking—either as their sole or supplemental activity—has little difficulty keeping the heart rate from becoming too high. More often than not, the reverse is the issue. The heart rate won't easily enter into the aerobic target zone. This happens for two reasons: the lower level of gravity-stress the walker is under and the fact that this stress is limited by the basic mechanics of walking. Nonetheless, the lower levels of intensity will provide the walker with numerous health and fitness benefits.

According to some studies, regular, easy physical exercise, such as walking, increases life expectancy. It also helps adults in their 60s, 70s and 80s maintain their functional independence—an important concern for society at large. Currently, the average number of nonfunctional years in America's elderly population averages almost 12. That's a long time to do nothing or to be unable to take care of oneself—let alone not enjoy life.

More specifically, consistent, low-output physical exercise can help in the prevention of and recovery from coronary disease—the leading cause of death in the United States. Physical activity is able to accomplish this in several ways. Besides improving the balance of blood fats, it increases the blood's clotting capacity and regulates blood sugars more efficiently. Furthermore, some studies associate regular exercise with lower incidents of colon cancer, stroke, and low back injury.

On the other hand, idle people invite the risk of coronary heart disease. In fact, inactivity—an independent risk factor related to heart problems—doubles the likelihood of having a cardiac episode.

It is possible to avoid this, as well as a host of other ailments, simply by walking for 30 minutes. Remember, we're talking here about placing one foot in front of the other in a leisurely fashion, not power or speed walking.

Unfortunately, statistics show that only 12 percent of the American population are willing to be even this active on a daily basis. And only 22 percent are willing to exercise this much five times a week.

Fig. 13.2. The FitMasta Heart FIT is fully water resistant. It has a mode for doing a 3-minute step test that determines the heart recovery rate. While the unit contains a clock, stopwatch and target zone settings, it does not offer the user any memory functions. (photo courtesy Atlantis International)

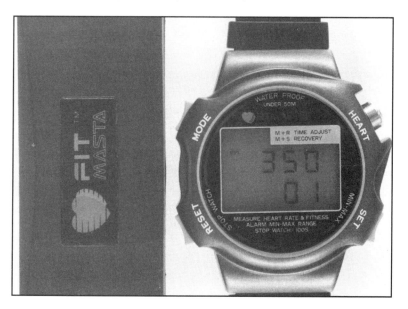

To make matters worse, our grade schools fail to assume a role in promoting physical activity for children. And this occurs despite the generally accepted knowledge that exercise improves academic achievement—not to mention its positive effect on a child's physical health and mental well-being.

All of the above issues have been noted by the American Academy of Pediatrics and the American College of Sports Medicine. Moreover, the United States Congress has passed a resolution (H. Cong. Res. 97) designed to encourage state and local educational agencies to include more physical education in the curriculums of students enrolled in grades K through 12.

Regrettably, to date only one state, Illinois, has complied. Worse than this report card has been the trend in schools not to promote physical education. Data from two periods (1974–1975 and 1984–1986) demonstrated a drop in that instruction from 36 percent to 33 percent.

Practice makes perfect, goes the old saw. And it seems that from an early age, America's children are perfecting the skill of doing little or nothing with their bodies. So, by the time they reach midlife, they're prone to being out of shape—if not in ill health. Walking is a good way to begin to reverse these inclinations.

Walking with the Heart Rate Monitor

If up until now your idea of a long walk is either from your car to the grocery store or from an easy chair to the refrigerator, one important caveat is in order. After you purchase some comfortable footwear and clothing, invest in a heart rate monitor. The device will prevent you from overtraining, a misfortune that plagues numerous athletes.

Despite the ease of walking, many of its practitioners— whether they're seasoned veterans or rank beginners—perform this activity at too high a heart rate. Why? Perhaps because of competitive feelings. Also, walking in a group encourages conversation—and, in case you don't know, talking may increase the heart rate.

Yet even solitary walkers can find their heart rates rising above the target zone should they ascend steep hills they're not fit enough to climb. So, ideally then, you want to curb competitive urges, keep heart rate–elevating chitchat to a minimum, and select terrain that suits your conditioning.

As for establishing a target zone that will keep you performing in an aerobic mode, adhere to the 180 formula that has been outlined in Chapter 5 Fundamentally, you will follow the same training rules that apply to cyclists, runners, and swimmers—including their warmup and cool-down periods.

There is one difference, though. You can reduce the lower target heart rate, if you want to. That means, instead of the normal 10-beat limit between the upper and lower heart rates in the target zone, you can lower the range by 20 beats. This reduction will assist novice walkers without detracting from the fat-burning aerobic process. So, if you determine that your maximum pulse is 135 bpm, make your base heart rate 20 beats less, or 115 bpm. Remember, the upper target zone ceiling remains the same.

Walking for Other Athletes

Walking offers competitive athletes, regardless of their disciplin, a valuable opportunity to improve their health and conditioning. Every competitive athlete can insert walking into their warmup and cool-down phases. Yet, all too frequently, serious exercisers believe these pre- and post-training routines are insignificant. One way to insure that you will warm up adequately is to walk 5 to 10 minutes prior to cycling, running, or swimming.

You can apply this same brief drill during the cool-down period. So, if you're a cyclist or swimmer, remember to bring along a pair of shoes you can comfortably wander about in. Many athletes who practice walking eventually say they don't feel "right" when they fail to do this.

Competitive athletes looking for an edge can gain one from walking. It will help promote recovery after a race or a strenuous workout. A moderate stroll for 20 to 30 minutes will gently increase the circulation of both the blood and lymph system—which speeds up the elimination of the body's waste products.

Athletes who view cross-training as a means of balancing their bodies and refreshing their psyches can devote one exercise segment exclusively to walking. During this workout, the heart rate should be kept at or below 80% of its aerobic maximum. For instance, if your pulse isn't supposed to go beyond 140 bpm, you don't want to raise it above 112 bpm. Bear in mind, you'll be walking from 45 minutes to an hour.

The positive, cross-training effect of this walking exercise is both muscular and neurological. (The nerves innervate specific muscle fibers.) And as previously mentioned, you'll be developing those small, aerobic muscle fibers that only come into play during very low intensity activities. Initially, many well-trained athletes who opt to walk report they feel some mild soreness upon concluding this seemingly effortless workout. Such minor discomfort is due to not using those small muscle fibers.

Besides developing these less active muscles, a walking session can rejuvenate the mind of a competitor who diligently adheres to one athletic discipline. As the training and racing season grinds on month after month, some athletes lose their enthusiasm for swimming, running, or cycling a bike.

Should this situation sound familiar, put a once-a-week walk into your training regimen. It can do wonders. Not only won't you lose any ground to your rivals, but you'll regain that old enthusiasm for your favorite activity. Who knows, walking could become so enjoyable that you might want to test yourself in competition.

Speed Walking

Generally, speed walkers fall into two categories owing to different gaits and walking postures. First, there is the normal walking style where where the walker, in the manner of a rush hour commuter, simply walks as fast as possible. Then there is the true race walk, known as the Olympic Walk, where the athlete's gait is quite distinct.

With arms rapidly pumping up and down, Olympic walkers adopt a striding style that ensures both feet don't leave the ground simultaneously. (Should that occur, they're in violation of a cardinal rule governing this international competition.) Undoubtedly, the sight of these walkers waddling along like a flock of frightened geese brings about derisive laughs. But while these athletes may look funny, a lot of runners would have their work cut out for them trying to stay on the walkers' tails.

Exercisers planning on competing in Olympic Walk events can effectively utilize the training information in this book. Follow the same fundamental rules for training, as well as the 180 formula to establish the appropriate heart rate. Don't forget to use the MAF test. It's a vital component for measuring progress, besides predicting and preventing a physical problem.

Unlike Olympic walking, which can stress the body, the style of most competitive walkers is quite ordinary. Still, these athletes do have to bend both arms at the elbows to make faster walking more efficient as well as more comfortable. It's a no-no, however, to exaggerate arm and shoulder movements; and, by all means, don't lengthen the leg-stride, either. All of these "unnatural" body movements can actually waste precious energy, in addition to raising the heart rate.

As you progress in your speed walk training program, you'll find your heart rate will no longer increase as much as when you first started. Don't worry. You're just becoming more proficient. In other words, as walkers get faster and faster at the same heart rates, they eventually won't be able to raise their pulses to their aerobic limits.

This comes about from the mechanics and stress (gravity) of walking, which retards the speed of the exerciser. Also, as a walker's fat-burning, aerobic metabolism grows more efficient, the heart rate doesn't need to rise as steeply. So, as you become more fit, you'll stride along at a higher speed with a correspondingly lower pulse.

Want to increase your workout intensity and bring your heart rate back up to its aerobic maximum again? It is as simple as carrying a lightweight dumbell in each hand. Hefting weights during a training walk increases mechanical stress, which, in turn, intensifies an aerobic workout. Yet it is a mistake to believe that once your hands are weight-free, you'll move with cheetah-like fleetness. The gains you'll make in speed will be marginal.

Assuming you want to carry weights around during a walk, pay strict attention to your heart rate; your pulse will rise in response to the extra burden. Start out with no more than a half pound in each hand. You may add another pound each time you see you're not getting any faster.

It is important to keep equal amounts of weight in both hands. Otherwise you are vulnerable to major mechanical stress. If you feel one hand is straining to bear a certain weight, don't clench your teeth and attempt to walk with it anyway. Clearly, this mass—no matter how light—is too heavy for your body.

While on the subject of training with weights, avoid employing those that wrap around the ankles. They create far too much physical stress for most walkers.

Ultimately, the value of ferrying about weights while walking has been blown way out of proportion. It is best to forget about pumping iron during training. Concentrate instead on piling up the miles, since walking is essentially an endurance activity.

Walking as Therapy

Walking is an unusually valuable therapy for athletes who want to take a break from rigorous training, such as exercisers in the throes of an injury.

Sometimes, when injury doesn't allow you to ride, run, or swim, you'll find you are able to go for a walk. If this gently aerobic activity doesn't cause further damage or pain, it is more beneficial than doing nothing.

There are instances, however, where walking could aggravate your injury. Should that be the case, you might want to try this: Head for the neighborhood swimming pool or lake and go through the walking motions in the water. Donning a flotation vest will insure that your feet won't touch the bottom.

Usually, walking is also a good means of returning to your favorite athletic activity after spending some time on the sideline, for whatever the reason. It enables you to gradually get back in gear without immediately jumping into high-level workouts.

So, whether you're young or old, a hard-nosed competitor or a recreational exerciser, don't dismiss the virtues of walking in your quest for fitness.

Chapter 14

Breathing: The Forgotten Component

When training or competing, all too many athletes fail to consider the way they are breathing. Like their non-athletic counterparts, they merely inhale and exhale in an unconscious manner. What both groups of people don't understand is that their heart rate will rise if they breathe incorrectly.

Is there really a right and a wrong way to breathe? Definitely. Only by breathing in accordance with the following pattern can you hope to reach optimum health and fitness:

☐ While inhaling, your abdominal muscles should be relaxed and gently pushed out, as you simultaneously extend the spine slightly.

☐ Exhalation calls for pulling in, or contracting, the abdominal muscles, as the spine is slightly flexed forward.

☐ The abdominals must be relaxed and extended during the inhalation. Throughout this process there is very little chest movement. Only during forced inhalation should the chest expand.

Most people, due to breathing habits developed in early childhood, use a breathing technique that is a far cry from this most effective pattern. When inhaling, their abdomen is pulled in and the chest rises; when exhaling, their chest falls and the abdomen heaves outward. This breathing style has a strong negative effect: The lungs exchange significantly less air during the inhalation-exhalation process. Over time, this can create a tremendous amount of stress on the body—and such stress becomes especially serious for the athlete while training or competing.

Here is a suggestion that will help you relearn how to breathe correctly:

Case History: Gordon's Energy

In all facets of life, Gordon was extremely disciplined. And he used this quality to get the most out of his bicycle training program. He always wore his HRM, ate the right food and, most important, he had carefully analyzed his abilities and objectives. Yet despite this balanced approach to exercising, he did have one significant problem: When competing, he gradually became so fatigued that he never had enough energy during the final miles to be a real threat at the finish line.

A quick observation revealed that Gordon wasn't breathing properly. It was suggested that he reverse his inhalation and exhalation patterns and then perform a series of exercises to strengthen the abdominal muscles. Since Gordon had been breathing incorrectly for 39 years, he initially experienced some difficulty making these adaptations. Yet he took a disciplined approach and mastered this crucial breathing rhythm in less than a month. This not only helped him become a top-10 contender, but it also improved his overall health and fitness.

☐ While standing, place your right hand on the middle of your abdomen. Put the left one on the thoraco-lumbar, i.e., the middle to lower section of the spine. Then slowly breathe in and out. Relax the abdominal muscles, allowing them to fall out on the inhalations and contract on the exhalations. Imagine that the space your hands surround is an empty vessel you are filling with air. Each morning and evening, devote 5–10 minutes to this practice for as long as it takes to get the hang of it.

Learning how to breathe correctly can be inhibited by a weak diaphragm muscle. To determine whether or not you have this problem, see how you do on these 3 simple self-examinations:

1. Breath Holding Time:
This test accurately measures the diaphragm's general capacity. Take a deep breath and see how long you can hold it. If you are in good health, you should be able to hold your breath for at least 50 seconds.

2. Snider's Test:
Relying on the power of breath, this test evaluates the diaphragm muscle's strength. Hold a lit match about 6 inches away from your mouth. With your mouth wide open, try to blow the flame out. If you have the slightest difficulty doing this, a problem may exist.

3. Vital Capacity:
In order to make this assessment, you will need a hand-held spirometer. Although this instrument cannot measure the rate of expired air, it can measure the amount of air (in cubic centimeters) that you can force out of your lungs. This number can be converted into a percentage of normal capacity as it relates to your height. On the spirometer's scale, which tops out at 120%, you should register somewhere between 55% and 110%. Studies show that vital capacity has a direct correlation

to a person's physiological age: The lower the vital capacity, the higher the physiological age, and vice versa.

If you score low on any of these 3 tests, you can strengthen your diaphragm muscle with a simple drill, the *straw exercise.* Place a straw in your mouth and breathe, in the correct pattern, for one or two minutes. Do this three times per week for two months, gradually working up to several two-minute sets. If you have a weak diaphragm, the straw exercise may prove difficult at first, but that should disappear after some practice.

Both a stronger diaphragm muscle and the correct breathing technique will make you much more efficient in your athletic endeavors. Your MAF, for example, can dramatically improve from one workout to the next, simply by extending the stomach outward when you take a breath. Another valuable dividend gained from breathing correctly is that you will be able to go faster at your normal heart rate.

Chapter 15

The Downside of Stretching

Most physical education teachers tell grade school children to do it. Many sports magazines publish articles about it. And countless athletes, regardless of their abilities, are dedicated to performing it.

Yes, it seems virtually everyone associated with athletics agrees it is mandatory to stretch—both before and after an event or workout. Otherwise, they feel there will be hell to pay in the form of aches and pains caused by tight muscles. Worse yet, warn trainers and coaches, you could tear some muscle fibers.

Much like the "no pain, no gain" axiom, stretching before and after exercising is based on tradition. And as with most customs, peoples' attitudes toward stretching are hard to reverse—especially when this routine is unequivocally espoused by coaches as well as elite athletes.

But is stretching really as valuable as many experts say it is? In truth, there is very little scientific information demonstrating the positive effects of touching your toes or pushing up against walls to extend taut quadriceps muscles. On the contrary. There is quite a lot of scientific evidence that shows stretching can actually be harmful.

For instance, Dr. Donald C. Murphy, the author of "A Critical Look at Static Stretching: Are we doing our patients harm?," (*Chiropractic Sports Medicine*, 5 (3), 1991) starts out by offering the different reasons individuals choose to stretch—and then reveals why most of these reasons are patently invalid.

As Murphy points out, the most common explanation for this pre- and post-exercise activity is to prevent pain or injury. Yet, he concludes there is very little documentation to confirm this widespread belief. Murphy goes on to cite several studies which conclude that static stretching can increase the risk of athletes hurting their bodies.

One of the salient examples he presents regards the hamstrings, a muscle group that athletes stretch frequently. It is also one of the muscle groups athletes frequently injure. The purpose of stretching the hamstrings is to increase flexibility, or the range of motion. Both goals are in the service of injury deterrence. But, as often as not, quite the opposite happens.

Ironically, stretching the hamstrings may cause them to become either tighter or hypoactive (decrease in muscle function), which may bring about a debilitating injury. Also, stretching can damage the inside of the muscle itself, the tendon and ligament that relates to the muscle, or even the joint that this muscle controls.

Even in light of scientific evidence, making a clean break with the tradition of stretching is a difficult task for most athletes. However, instead of engaging in this customary activity, you can reap greater benefits by adhering to the warmup and cool-down routines that gradually raise and lower the heart rate. Both of these practices will make you more flexible.

Chapter 16

The Effect of Altitude

Training and competing at altitudes above 3,000 ft (1,000 m) increases the level of stress on an athlete's body, a factor that is particularly relevant in cycling. However, using an HRM to tackle an arduous ascent can overcome this problem.

Riding in the mountains is dramatically different from riding at sea level. Not only do you have to work harder, but your breathing also becomes noticeably more difficult. Breathing becomes more of a problem at elevation because the atmospheric pressure is lower in this environment. As a result, the body takes in less oxygen. When this happens, it takes more effort to do the same amount of work—which is indicated by a marked rise in your "normal" heart rate.

And since most cyclists train by quantity (miles) rather than quality (intensity), their higher heart rates can lead to more injuries—both structural and biochemical—while they are riding at elevation. Frequently, a rider's response to this situation is to become depressed or anxious. In part, this emotional state is due to the increased production of lactic acid associated with the lower oxygen uptake. (It is well known that higher lactic acid levels can trigger such changes in temperament.)

Unfortunately, many cyclists who relocate to train in the mountains base this move on a questionable assumption. Originally, it was believed that the body, responding to the decreased oxygen uptake at higher elevations, produced an increased number of red blood cells. It has proven very

Case History: Brian's Adjustments

Brian, 25, was making incredible progress as a competitive cyclist. In fact, he had rapidly become one of the best racers on the eastern seaboard. Because he was a high school teacher, he could devote his entire summer to training and competing. In order to make some real fitness gains, he decided to head for the mountains, and went to Boulder, Colorado.

This cycling mecca, complete with name riders and awesome landscape, had the desired affect: Brian redoubled his commitment to train harder. With the altitude elevating his heart rate, Brian pushed himself to keep up with the local hot-shots. As a result of these two new stresses, he destroyed the healthy state of his mind and body. Brian's leg muscles convulsed with muscle spasms and, unable to ride, he was overcome by depression.

An agonizing telephone conversation with his sports medicine doctor produced the same advice Brian had received before departing: He was reminded to pay close attention to his heart rate readings and stick to the same training program that had produced a high level of achievement before.

After spending three weeks training alone, Brian's health and performance dramatically improved. Eventually, he rode with the pack again—but only during aerobic workouts. On the days that called for anaerobic intervals, Brian either did them by himself or with a couple of riders whose abilities matched his.

Upon returning to the east coast at the end of the summer, Brian had the kind of race results that most cyclists can only dream about.

difficult, however, to assert this hypothesis with certainty. A study conducted in 1986 by Dr. Robert Glover at the University of Colorado has raised some fascinating questions about red blood cell production. His research clearly demonstrated that red blood cells do not significantly increase in number when an individual is at high altitudes. Furthermore, Dr. Glover discovered that at elevation, plasma levels are lowered as a result of leakage from circulation. This escaping plasma tends to promote a more concentrated population of red blood cells which, in turn, creates the *appearance* of higher numbers. Still, proper training in the mountains may provide benefits to the cyclist.

To insure the chances of this occurring, the body must be given a reasonable period to adapt to the added stress of living and riding at altitude. So athletes hoping to improve their conditioning will have to spend 2 to 3 weeks acclimatizing to this new environment.

An HRM will remove the guesswork from your adaptation process. By wearing the device when both on as well as off the bicycle, you can remain aware of the essential triad of heart rate information: your morning pulse, your resting pulse, and your MAF in the target zone. Initially, all three of these parameters will probably be slightly higher than normal.

The time required for these readings to stabilize depends on your degree of fitness. Upon adjusting to your alpine surroundings, you will begin to make conditioning advances. These improvements, though, will be similar to the gains you can attain at sea level. But should you travel above 10,000 feet, expect to have some trouble making gains in your fitness. At this height, oxygen uptake is dramatically lower than at sea level.

Eventually, after coming down from the mountains, you will have developed a marked increase in your oxygen uptake. Dropping from 1,863 meters to sea level, for example, will increase oxygen uptake by 11.1 percent. A decent of 3,000 meters increases the total oxygen uptake by nearly 18 percent. Corresponding incremental jumps in fitness would usually require many months—or years—of training on a daily basis. Yet, even if all goes well for you while training at altitude, don't expect this kind of change to take place immediately upon descending. It will require about 3 weeks to achieve such a peak conditioning experience.

To verify any improvements in oxygen uptake, check your MAF. Racers, in particular, should make careful note of this aforementioned sequence: adaptation, training, descending, and peaking. Failure to accurately account for the days needed to meet this schedule could mean that you won't derive oxygen uptake benefits in time for a specific competition. Remember, just riding at altitude will not automatically enhance your training program. You must pay strict attention to your bodily changes. And when it comes to obtaining this essential information, there's no better tool than an HRM.

Chapter 17

The HRM in Injury Prevention and Rehabilitation

Nothing can be more frustrating to a dedicated athlete than sustaining a serious injury or illness that curtails his or her workouts or competition. Athletes know all too well that a malady that interferes with their activity for several weeks —or months—will engender a loss of fitness. Often, people faced with this prospect become either mildly depressed or ridden with anxiety.

One of the major underlying themes of this volume is that an HRM, when used correctly, can prevent many sports-related injuries. Moreover, in certain instances, the HRM can be used as a therapeutic device to help you get back on your feet after an injury or illness. And, lastly, it can help you prevent common physical maladies.

Many injuries that plague athletes are caused by overtraining. As previously mentioned, this phenomenon can easily be prevented by using an HRM to train in the target zone, and to check your morning and resting pulse levels.

But let's say you are beleaguered by an overtraining injury before you start using an HRM. How can you use the device to get your body back on the right track? Simple: As noted in Chapter 5, when computing the target zone numbers, you must take an injury into consideration. Having done that, train within this parameter for 2 or 3 weeks. If your injury does not heal within this period, you will have to make two important modifications to facilitate your rehabilitation:

Should your injury allow you to exercise—even if just for 20 minutes—modifying the target zone downward (see below) should restore you to good health again. If, on the other hand, you feel aches and pains only when working out for more than an hour, it's crucial not to exceed this limit, as well

---

Case History: Mark's Intuition

Mark was completely satisfied with his training program. What pleased him most was that for the first time in several years he had been able to ride the entire season totally free of excruciating sciatic pain. Mark attributed this good fortune to paying close attention to his HRM. He became so sensitive to this training partner that he knew exactly what his pulse would be even before looking at the numbers displayed on the receiver.

After three years of daily use, the battery in Mark's HRM finally failed. He decided not to replace this small, inexpensive item but, instead, relied on his "intuition" to assess his pulse.

Within four months of intuitive training, Mark was jolted by a severe sciatic episode. One morning, when the pain in his leg was particularly acute, he called his sports physician to arrange an appointment. Instead of seeing Mark, the doctor offered the following advice: Replace the HRM's battery, lower the target zone range 10 bpm, and then spend a few days on the bike only spinning during workouts.

Two days later, Mark felt no discomfort and was able to resume his normal training regimen.

---

as to make a target zone readjustment. (Of course, the HRM is not a panacea. If you experience pain or discomfort the moment you start exercising, this indicates a need to see a health professional.) For both of the above examples, here is the procedure for the proper heart rate adjustments:

☐ Using your present target zone as a guide, employ the lower number as the new high number of the modified range. Then subtract 10 from this lower number to arrive at the new base figure of your target zone. For example, if your normal aerobic training range happens to be 140 bpm to 150 bpm, alter this down to 130–140 for the rehabilitation period. The length of time you should maintain this new target rate will be explained below.

☐ Extend the warmup and cool-down periods by 50 percent while you are working out in the rehabilitation phase. That means each of the usual 15-minute sessions should be increased to at least 22 minutes. If your regular warmup and cool-down phases are of longer duration, change both of them accordingly.

Rehabilitation Time

When injured, some athletes tend to adopt a macho attitude. With teeth clenched and a grimace on their face, they will continue training until it truly becomes physically impossible. Others respond to pain and discomfort by becoming over-cautious. For them, the mere sight of a blister is a reason to give up.

Both of these psychological dispositions will do little to restore you to a healthy condition. To totally disregard an injury could very well compound its severity. And while rest and relaxation can help the body heal itself, it can be extremely stressful for an athlete to assume a totally inactive stance. Should you be faced with an injury, be sensible and adopt a middle-of-the-road attitude: Adjust your target zone down, and then proceed with caution.

All athletes experiencing physical problems invariably ask the same question: How long will it take me to get better? The time frame for the restoration of health, obviously, varies with each case. Still, here is a general guideline: After revising the target zone to its rehabilitation range, begin exercising at that level for no more than 3 weeks. Resume training at the normal aerobic heart rate if there is a noticeable improvement at end of this period. Assuming that a relapse of any kind does not occur, you can continue with your regular training program.

Unfortunately, sometimes the rehabilitation process will not go so smoothly. Upon returning to the normal target zone, the injury may flare up again, leading to a disappointing regression. Don't lose heart: Immediately change the target zone back to its rehabilitation parameters and train at that level for another 3 weeks. Sometimes, this aerobic modification period still won't do the trick. When that happens, continue in this modified zone for another 3 weeks.

If you are not improving—or are feeling worse—after this 6-week rehabilitation segment, you should consult a health professional.

Preventing and Recovering from Illness

Even the most finely tuned athletic "machine" may come down with sniffles, a cold or the flu. When this happens, your body's metabolism increases to fight off and recover from this annoying or disabling invader. Usually, the struggle for the restoration of good health will raise your normal heart rate.

If you do notice a rise in your resting and active heart rates, it is best to stop working out for one or two days. Failure to do so could lower your body's defenses and allow the illness to get a good grip on your system.

Should your ailment be accompanied by a fever, definitely don't exercise. When your temperature rises above 98.6°F

Case History: Judy's Overtraining Injury

For the third consecutive year, Judy had a great competitive cycling season. But there was one problem: For the first time, an injury forced her to miss a race. Worse still, her next race — an important event at the end of her race calendar— proved to be disastrous from a performance standpoint.

To rectify this shattering race result, Judy trained harder over the winter. By spring, she was in excellent shape—but her injuries reappeared, and she was unable to participate in any early season contests.

It was recommended that Judy devote four months to building a solid aerobic base. She was reluctant to follow this advice because she didn't want to spend so much time doing only "easy" training rides. In the end, since she had run out of options, she decided to go along with the base-building program.

By early summer Judy's endurance and aerobic speed had improved significantly. In her first criterium, which marked the beginning of the anaerobic phase of training, she performed much better than she had hoped for. Throughout the summer, Judy's race results continued to improve and by the end of October she was eager to begin her long base period.

(37°C), your metabolism is racing and, therefore, your heart rate will be elevated. You can resume training as soon as you are fever-free for 24 hours and your morning heart rate is within 3 beats of its normal reading.

After getting back to training, you may feel good enough to perform a strenuous workout. Resist this temptation. Remember, your body is still recuperating from an illness. To jump aggressively back into your training routine could cause a serious relapse. The way to avoid this possibility is to spend 2 or 3 days exercising with your target zone reduced by 10 bpm. So, if your regular range is 135–145, reduce the span to 125–135. This conservative approach should bring your morning heart rate down to normal, which indicates that you're ready to train hard again.

Although these remedial procedures are simple enough, some athletes will not adopt them for fear that a couple of days resting, or at least not going full blast, will provide their competitors with an edge. Ultimately, a more serviceable approach harmonizes the desire for peak conditioning and the need for good health.

Chapter 18

Conclusion

"Even the longest journey begins with the first step," states the Tao Te Ching, the Chinese book of proverbs. The first step to improving both your health and fitness is taking the time to exercise regularly. In order to sustain a high level of enthusiasm, here are some simple suggestions to follow.

First, establish realistic objectives. There are numerous reasons to start an exercise program—becoming fitter, losing weight, or becoming the first person on your block to win the New York marathon or the Tour de France's yellow jersey. Regardless of your avowed purpose, take an objective look at your circumstances. If you're 6 ft. 4 in. and tip the scales at 250 pounds, it's highly unlikely that you'll become a "King of the Mountain." Moreover, at age 45, don't expect to develop the cardiovascular capacity of Ironman Mark Allen or 3-time Tour de France victor Greg Lemond. And even if you are 19 years old and in phenomenal shape, your chances of defeating a world-class athlete are very slight.

All this is not to say that you shouldn't bring high aspirations to your training program. However, it's advisable to be ruthlessly honest with yourself about the physical material you are working with. Just remember, you can reach your full athletic potential and become healthier by consistently working out with an HRM.

Still, some athletes become so obsessed with becoming fitter and winning races that they create conflicts at home, at school, or in the workplace. Before designing and committing yourself to an exercise program, consider how it will effect your primary obligations. A well-conceived training and competition agenda should not interfere with your daily existence.

Second, maintain a diary. Each day, take the time to record the following information: your morning pulse, high and low heart rates for each training or competitive event, and a few comments that characterize your performance (the type of activity, times, placing, how you felt). These notations will provide you with invaluable data about your progress, plateaus, and regressions. By carefully analyzing this record, you can make the necessary adjustments that will promote your overall well-being.

Third, when training, discard the anachronistic athletic axiom "no pain, no gain." Upon the completion of an aerobic workout that has been performed correctly, you should feel like you have enough energy to perform it again—immediately. If you finsh a training session feeling totally wasted, chances are you have been overexerting yourself. Although this intense effort can raise your pain threshold, the fundamental purpose of exercising is to preserve a bodily balance between health and fitness.

Both health and conditioning are clearly lifelong endeavors. Still, each day that you train will generate immediate benefits. Not only will you look and feel better, but you will also have more energy, as well as the capacity to be more productive. These worthwhile goals are clearly attainable by working out with a heart rate monitor.

Appendix

Heart Rate Monitor Contacts

ACT
(708) 491-9628

Biosig Instruments
(514) 637-0016

Cat Eye
(816) 719-7781

Creative Health Products
(Free HRM Buyer's Guide)
1-800-279-2820

Elexis Corporation
(305) 592-6069

FitMasta
(203) 226-2394

Fuji America
1-800-631-8474

Nissei
1-800-742-4478

Polar USA
1-800-227-1314

Schwinn Bicycle Company
(708) 231-5340

Seca

1-800-356-1696

Sensor Dynamics, Inc.

1-800-764-4327

Vetta

(818) 780-8808

Bibliography

Aerobic & Anaerobic

1. Martin, D. W. et al. *Harpers Review of Biochemistry,* Los Altos, CA: Lange Med. Pub., 1985.

2. McArdle, W. D., F. I. Katch, and V. L. Katch. *Exercise Physiology* (3rd ed.). Philadelphia: Lea & Febiger, 1991.

3. Bjorntorp, P. "Importance of Fat as a Support Nutrient for Energy." *J. Sp. Sci., 9*: Spec No. 71-6, Summer 1991.

4. Astrand, P. O., and K. Rodahl. *Textbook of Work Physiology*. New York: McGraw-Hill, 1977.

5. Gollnick, P. D., and L. Hermansen. *Biochemical Adaptations to Exercise: Anaerobic Metabolism*, Volume I. New York: Academic Press, 1973.

6. Brodal, A. *Anatomy in Relation to Clinical Medicine*. New York: Oxford University Press, 1981.

7. Cohen, M. E., F. C. Consolazio, and R. E. Johnson. "Blood Lactate Response During Moderate Exercise in Neurocirculatory Asthenia, Anxiety Neurosis, or Effort Syndrome." *Journal of Clinical Investigation*: 339–342, 1947.

8. Gorman, J. M., M. R. Liebowitz, and D. F. Klein. "Panic Disorder and Agoraphobia." *Diagnostic and Statistical Manual of Mental Disorders* (3rd ed.). Washington, DC: American Psychiatric Association, 1980.

9. Pitts, F. N., Jr., and J. N. McClure, Jr. "Lactate Metabolism in Anxiety Neurosis." *New England Journal of Medicine*: 1329–1336, 1967.

10. Conconi, Francesco, et al. "Determination of the Anaerobic Threshold by a Noninvasive Field Test in Runners." *Cattedra di Biochemica Applicata*. Ferrera, Italy, 1980.

11. Dimsdale, J. E., and J. Moss. "Plasma Catecholamines in Stress and Exercise." *Journal of the American Medical Association*: 340–342, 1980.

12. Grimby, G., et al. "Cardiac Output During Submaximal and Maximal Exercise in Active Middle-Aged Athletes." *Journal of Applied Physiology,* 21:1150, 1966.

13. Hennerman, E., and C. Olson. "Relations between Structure and Function in the Design of Skeletal Muscles." *J. Neurophysiology,* 28:581, 1985.

14. Mountcastle, V. B. *Medical Physiology* (13th ed.), Volumes I and II. St. Louis: C.V. Mosby, 1974.

15. Leaf, D. A. et al. "Respiratory Exchange Ratio Slope: A new concept in the determination of physical fitness and exercise training." *Annals of Sports Medicine, 3:* 210–214, 1988.

16. Selye, Hans, M.D. *The Stress of Life.* New York: McGraw-Hill, 1956.

17. Kindermann et al. "The Relationship of Heart Rate, Lactate, and Maximum Oxygen Uptake and Expired Air." *European Journal of Applied Physiology,* 42:25–35, 1979

Fueling the Aerobic & Anaerobic Systems, combined with Carbohydrates and Insulin

1. Keller, K., et al. "Pre-exercise Snacks May Decrease Exercise Performance." *Phys. Sportsmed., 12:* 89, 1984.

2. Wolever, T. M., et al. "Effect of Psyllium on Glucose response." *J. Am. Coll. Nutrition,* 10(4):364–71, Aug 1991.

3. Thomas, D. E., et al. "Carbohydrate Feeding Before Exercise: Effect of glycemic index." *International Journal of Sports Medicine,* 12(2):80–186, Apr 1991.

4. Jenkins, D. J. A., et al. "Glycemic Index of Foods: A physiological basis for carbohydrate exchange." *Am. J. Clin. Nutr.,* 34:362–366, 1981.

5. Berkow, R. *Merck Manual.* Rahway, NJ: Merck Res. Labs, 1992.

6. Bassett, D. R., et al. "Recognition of Borderline Carbohydrate-Lipid Metabolism Disturbance: An incipient form of type IV hyperlipoproteinemia?" *J. Cardiovasc. Pharmacology,* 15 (Suppl. 5):S8–17, 1990.

7. Levine, L., et al. "Fructose and Glucose Ingestion and Muscle Glycogen Use During Submaximal Exercise." *Journal of Applied Physiology, 55*:1767–1771, 1983.

8. Martin, D. W., et al. *Harpers Review of Biochemistry*, Los Altos, CA: Lange Med. Pub., 1985.

9. McArdle, W. D., F. I. Katch, and V. I. Katch. *Exercise Physiology* (3rd ed.). Philadelphia: Lea & Febiger, 1991.

10. Costill, D. L., et al. "Effects of Elevated Plasma Free Fatty Acids and Insulin on Muscle Glycogen Usage During Exercise." *Journal of Applied Physiology, 43*:695–699, 1977.

11. Reaven, G. M. "Role of Insulin Resistance in Human Disease." *Diabetes, 37*:1595–1607, 1988.

12. Fuh, M. D., et al. "Abnormalities of Carbohydrate and Lipid Metabolism in Patients with Hypertension." *Arch. Intern. Med., 147*:1035–1038, 1987.

13. Bjorntorp, P. "Importance of Fat as a Support Nutrient for Energy." *J. Sp. Sci., 9*: Spec No:71–6, Summer 1991.

14. Burr, G. O., and M. M. Burr. *Journal of Biological Chemistry, 82*: 345–367, 1929.

15. *Essential Fatty Acids and Prostaglandins.* Creative Audio Tapes. 8751 Osburne, Highland, IN 46322, 1982.

16. Moser, M., and R. Gorlin. "Comments on the Report from the National Cholesterol Education Program." *Primary Cardiology,* April 1988.

17. Oscal, L. B. "Exercise and Lipid Metabolism." *Progress in Clinical and Biological Research, 67*:383–390, 1981.

18. Mountcastle, V. B. *Medical Physiology* (13th ed.), Volume II. St. Louis: C.V. Mosby, 1970.

19. *Nutrition Reviews: Present Knowledge in Nutrition.* New York: The Nutrition Foundation, 1976.

20 Orten, J. M., and O. W. Neuhaus. *Biochemistry.* St. Louis: C.V. Mosby, 1970.

21. Barnes, B. O., and C. W. Barnes. *Heart Attack Rareness in Thyroid-Treated Patients.* Springfield, IL: Charles Thomas, 1973.

22. Erasmus, U. *Fats and Oils.* Vancouver, BC: Alive Books, 1986.

23. Moore, T. J. *Heart Failure*. New York: Simon & Schuster, 1989.

Training

1. Martin, D. W., et al. *Harpers Review of Biochemistry*. Los Altos, CA: Lange Med. Pub., 1985.

2. McArdle, W. D., F. I. Katch, and V. I. Katch. *Exercise Physiology*. (3rd ed.). Philadelphia: Lea & Febiger, 1991.

3. Holloszy, J., et al. "Adaptations of Skeletal Muscle to Endurance Exercise and their Metabolic Consequences." *Journal of Applied Physiology, 56*:831–838, 1984.

4. Simoneau, J., et al. "Human Skeletal Muscle Fiber Type Alteration with High-Intensity Intermittent Training. *Eur. J. Appl. Physiology, 54*:250–253, 1985.

3. Turnstall-Pedoe, D. "Exercise and Sudden Death." *British Journal Sports Medicine, 12*:215–219, 1979.

4. Maffetone, P. *Everyone Is an Athlete*. David Barmore Productions (Box 785, Mahopac, NY 10505), 1990.

5. Bailey, C. *Fit or Fat*. Boston: Houghton Mifflin, 1978.

6. Lydiard, A. (with Garth Gilmout). *Running With Lydiard*. London: Hodder and Stoughton, 1983.

Physical fitness and walking

1. Paffenbarger, R. S., et al. "Physical Activity, All-Cause Mortality, and Longevity of College Alumni." *New England Journal of Medicine, 314*:605–613, 1986.

2. Katz, S., et al. "Active Life Expectancy." *New England Journal of Medicine, 309*:1218–1224, 1983.

3. Harris, S. S., et al. "Physical Activity Counseling for Healthy Adults as a Primary Preventive Intervention in the Clinical Setting. *Journ. A.M.A., 261*:3590–3598, 1989.

4. Powell, K. E., et al. "Physical Activity and Chronic Disease." *American Journal of Clinical Nutrition, 49*:999–1006, 1989.

5. Salonen, J.T., P. Puska, and J. Tuomilehto. "Physical Activity and Risk of Myocardial Infarction, Cerebral Stroke and Death: A longitudinal study in Eastern Finland." *American Journal of Epidemiology, 115*:526–537, 1982.

6. Cady, L. D., et al. "Strength and Fitness and Subsequent Back Injuries in Firefighters." *Journal of Occupational Medicine, 21*:269–272, 1979.

Warming Up and Cooling Down

1. Saltin, B. " Aerobic Work Capacity and Circulation at Exercise in Man With Special Reference to the Effect of Prolonged Exercise and/or Heat Exposure." *Actua Physilogium Scandinavia:* 1–52, 1964.

2. Martin, D. W., et al. *Harpers Review of Biochemistry.* Los Altos, CA: Lange Med. Pub., 1985.

3. McArdle, W. D., F. I. Katch, and V. I. Katch. *Exercise Physiology* (3rd ed.). Philadelphia: Lea & Febiger, 1991.

Altitude training

1. Wyndam, C. H., et al. "Physiological Effects of Acute Changes in Altitude in a Deep Mine." *Journal of Applied Physiology, 36*:399–402, 1974.

2. Rosen, S. *Weathering.* New York: M. Evans, 1979.

3. Gamow, R. I. *Hyperbaric Mountain Bag Instruction Manual.* Boulder, CO, 1988.

4. Linnarsson, D., et al. "Muscle Metabolites and Oxygen Deficit with Exercise in Hypoxia and Hyperoxia. *Journal of Applied Physiology, 36*:399–402, 1974.

Injury & Rehabilitation

1. Kendall, F. P., and E. K. McCreary. *Muscle Testing and Function* (3rd ed.). Baltimore: Williams & Wilkins, 1983.

2. Walther, D. S. *Applied Kinesiology Synopsis*. Pueblo, CO:
    Systems DC, 1988.

3. Walther, D. S. *Applied Kinesiology, V*olume I. Pueblo, CO: Systems
    DC, 1981.

4. International College of Applied Kinesiology. *Status Statement.*
    Box 25276, Shawnee Mission, Kansas 66225, USA.

5. Liesman, G., P. Shambaugh, and A. Ferentz. "Somatosensory
    Evoked Potential Changes During Muscle Testing." *International
    Journal of Neuroscience, 45*:143-151, 1989.

Index

Other Titles Available from Bicycle Books

Title	Author	US Price
All Terrain Biking	Jim Zarka	$7.95
The Backroads of Holland	Helen Colijn	$12.95
The Bicycle Repair Book	Rob van der Plas	$9.95
Bicycle Repair Step by Step (color)*	Rob van der Plas	$14.95
Bicycle Technology	Rob van der Plas	$16.95
Bicycle Touring International	Kameel Nasr	$18.95
The Bicycle Touring Manual	Rob van der Plas	$16.95
Bicycling Fuel	Richard Rafoth, M.D.	$9.95
Cycling Canada	John Smith	$12.95
Cycling Europe	Nadine Slavinski	$12.95
Cycling France	Jerry Simpson	$12.95
Cycling Kenya	Kathleen Bennett	$12.95
Cycling the San Francisco Bay Area	Carol O'Hare	$12.95
Cycling the U.S. Parks	Jim Clark	$12.95
A Guide to Cycling Injuries*	Domhnal McAuley	$12.95
In High Gear (hardcover)	Samuel Abt	$21.95
The High Performance Heart	Maffetone & Mantell	$10.95
The Mountain Bike Book	Rob van der Plas	$10.95
Mountain Bike Magic (color)	Rob van der Plas	$14.95
Mountain Bike Maintenance (color)	Rob van der Plas	$10.95
Mountain Bikes: Maint. & Repair*	Stevenson & Richards	$22.50
Mountain Bike Racing (hardcover)*	Burney & Gould	$22.50
The New Bike Book	Jim Langley	$4.95
Roadside Bicycle Repairs (color)	Rob van der Plas	$7.95

Buy our books from a book store or bike shops

We and our distributors can supply any of these books to the trade. However, if you have difficulty obtaining our books locally, we will be pleased to supply them by mail, but we must add $2.50 postage and handling (and California Sales Tax if mailed to a California address). For Priority Mail, add $1.00 per book. Prepayment by check or credit card must be included with your order. For foreign orders, postage will be added at actual cost.

Bicycle Books, Inc.
1282 - 7th Avenue
San Francisco CA 94122
Tel. (415) 665-8214 or 1-800-468-8233

In Britain: Bicycle Books
463 Ashley Road
Poole, Dorset BH14 0AX
Tel. (01202) 71 53 49

---

* Books marked thus not available from Bicycle Books in the U.K.